(IMPROVED)

Compiled by C. R. Nichol and Wife

Enlarged by
C. R. Nichol and J. W. Denton

Go ye into
all the w**O**rld and preach
the go**S**pel to every creature. He that
believeth and is ba**P**tized shall be
sav**E**d; but he that believeth not
shal**L** be damned.—Mk. 16:15-16.

Go
ye theref**O**re, and teach
all nation**S**
ba**P**tizing them
in the nam**E** of the Father, and the
Son, and of the Ho**L**y Ghost.— Matt. 28:19.

A·C·U
PRESS

A. C. U. PRESS
Abilene Christian University
1648 Campus Court
ABILENE, TEXAS 79601

ISBN 0-915547-55-4

CONTENTS

THE BIBLE

The word "Bible" is from the Greek *Biblos,* meaning *a book.* Being a revelation of the will of God to the human family, it is pre-eminently *The Book.*

About forty persons were engaged in writing the Bible. The first was Moses, the last John.

About 1500 years were consumed in writing the Bible.

The Bible is composed of the Old and New Testaments.

Testament means *will* or *agreement.*

There are three dispensations recognized in the Bible, viz. (1st) The Patriarchal—from Adam to Moses; (2nd) the Jewish—from Moses to the death of Christ, and (3rd) the Christian—from Pentecost to the end of the world.

The Old Testament was written, most of it in the Hebrew, though some was written in Chaldaic.

The New Testament was written in Greek.

The Bible has been translated into the prominent languages of earth.

The "King James" translation—the one most frequently used—was made in 1606-1611.

The Revised Version was made in 1885.

The Old Testament, with its thirty-nine books, was written by not fewer than thirty persons. All were Israelites, save Job, who was a sage of Idumea.

The Old Testament is arranged into four departments, viz.: (1st) The Pentateuch, (2nd) History, (3rd) Poetry, (4th) Prophecy.

Pentateuch is from *Pente*, five, and *Teuchos*, a volume, and means the five-fold volume, viz.: Gen., Ex., Lev., Num. and Deut. The first five books are also called "The Book of the Law of Moses," Neh. 8:1; "The Book of the Law of Jehovah," Neh. 9:3.

Moses is the author of the Pentateuch.

Significance of the Names of the Pentateuch: The word "Genesis" is from the Greek word *genesis*, which means *origin*, or *beginning*, hence it is the Book of Beginning.

"Exodus" is from the Greek word *exodus*, and means *exit* or *departure*. It is the Book of Departure, and contains the history of the departure of the children of Israel from Egypt.

Leviticus is from "Levi," a son of Jacob. The priests were his descendants. Leviticus is the book of the Priesthood.

Numbers. So called because it contains the history of the numbering of the children of Israel at two different times.

Deuteronomy is from *deuteros*, second, and *nomos, law*, and signifies "Second Law." Not a second law, nor a new law, but a restating of the law given at Sinai.

In the Pentateuch you find the history of the creation, the destruction of the wicked by the flood, the choosing of a special people, the schooling of them in Egypt and the wilderness, the giving of the law from Sinai, and the system of worship for Patriarchal and Jewish age.

Historical Books

Joshua. So called from its author, Joshua, the successor of Moses. It contains a history of the crossing of the Jordan, taking of the land of Canaan and giving of each tribe their part of the land.

Judges. Most likely Samuel is its author. It contains the history of the Israelites after the death of Joshua, and history through the reign of thirteen Judges.

Ruth. This is rather a supplement to the book of Judges, written, it is thought, by Samuel.

1 and 2 Samuel. Here you will find the history of Samuel, the anointing of Saul and David, and the death of Saul.

1 and 2 Kings. History of the reign of Solomon. The division of Israel.

1 and 2 Chronicles. History of the reign of Solomon and the captivity of Judah. Written by Ezra.

Ezra. Named after its author, Ezra. Contains the history of the return from captivity and the rebuilding of the temple.

Nehemiah. The history of the building of the walls of Jerusalem against the opposition of the heathen.

Esther. The book is named after the principal character mentioned in it—Esther. It tells of God's protection of the Jews, though scattered among the heathens. Possibly Mordecai is the author.

Poetical Books

Job. A history of the afflictions of Job and his steadfastness.

Psalms. A collection of sacred songs and poems, as well as many prophecies.

Proverbs. Code of ethics or rules of life.

Ecclesiastes. The name is from a Greek word, meaning a *preacher*. Solomon is the author. Here you will find the history of a failure to be happy if you pander to worldly pomp and carnality.

Song of Solomon.

Prophetical Books

Isaiah. Sometimes called the "Evangelical Prophet" or the "Gospel Prophet," because of the many predictions relative to the coming of Christ and the work he would do for the race.

Jeremiah. Here you will find the prediction of many things that were to befall Judah, and that they would return after seventy years.

Lamentations, by Jeremiah. His grief expressed because of the destruction of Jerusalem and the temple.

Ezekiel. Predictions of the evil that would befall Judah, the complete destruction of Jerusalem and the temple, and the return from Babylonian captivity.

Daniel. Tells of the development and fall of the kingdoms of this world and the triumph of the Kingdom of God.

Hosea. Denounces Israel for their unfaithfulness and tells of the captivity they would suffer.

Joel. Predicts that enemies will invade the country, and foretells the outpouring of the Holy Spirit.

Amos. He predicts evil for the nations around Israel, and declares that Israel and Judah would not escape punishment for their sins.

Obadiah. Israel is assured of blessings, though they were to suffer much from the nations about them.

Jonah. The adventure and deliverance of Jonah. His preaching at Nineveh.

Micah. Declares that the Christ would be born, and is very explicit as to the place.

Nahum. Tells of the goodness of God. The destruction of Nineveh is foretold minutely; with a description of how the army would enter the city.

Habakkuk. In this book you will find a description of how wicked the people had become, and the promise of God that the time would come when he would be glorified in the earth.

Zephaniah. A denunciation of the people for their wickedness and a call to them to repentance.

Haggai. Encourages the people to work in rebuilding the temple, with the assurance that the temple rebuilt would have more glory than formerly.

Zechariah. The rebuilding of the temple. The promise of a "priest and King" who was the Christ.

Malachi. He reproves the people and their teachers for their sins, and declares to them that punishment will certainly be theirs if they do not repent.

THE NEW TESTAMENT

The New Testament was written by eight men—six apostles and two evangelists.

It may be arranged into four divisions: (1st) Biography, (2nd) History, (3rd) Didactical, (4th) Prophecy.

Matthew was written by Matthew, one of the early disciples, who was also one of the apostles.

Mark. He traveled with Paul and Barnabas on a missionary tour, but was not one of the apostles.

Luke. A companion of Paul.

John. The "beloved disciple." He is the only one of the apostles that was not martyred.

These four historians give us the account of the birth, life, work, trial, crucifixion, burial, resurrection, and ascension of Christ.

Acts of Apostles. Written by Luke. Here is given the history of the ascension of Christ, selection of Matthias, the baptism of the apostles in the Holy Spirit, establishment of the church of Christ, with its growth, and persecution of the disciples. It may also be styled the book of conversions. It contains the history of the preaching in and around Jerusalem, as well as some of the missionary journeys they made.

Romans. Written by Paul to the church of Christ at Rome. In it you find the power of the gospel mentioned, how sinful men had become, grace and works—the law and the gospel—contrasted. Why the Jews were rejected and the conditions on which they may be saved. Our attitude towards the civil powers.

1 Corinthians. By Paul. The sinfulness of division among the people of God. Reproof of those who sin. Withdrawing from those who will not live right. Lord's Supper. Spiritual gifts. The "More Excellent Way." Resurrection of the dead.

2 Corinthians. By Paul. The excellencies of the gospel over the law. Assurance of immortal glory for the faithful. The grace of giving of your means for the spread of the gospel.

Galatians. By Paul. These people had been converted from worshiping idols to Judaism, and then to Christianity. There was a disposition on the part of some of them to return to Judaism. The letter warns them of such a course and presents the superiority of the gospel over the law.

Ephesians. By Paul. The purpose of God. Redemption of man. Salvation by grace. Good works. Gentiles object of salvation. Duty of children to parents. The Christian life compared to a warfare.

Philippians. By Paul. Philippi was the chief city of Macedonia. It was there Paul and Silas were imprisoned. This church had expressed sympathy for Paul in his missionary work, and contributed to his support. He expresses his appreciation and warns them against false teachers.

Colossians. By Paul. Exhortation to faithfulness. Warning against traditions and ordinances of the law.

1 Thessalonians. By Paul. Timothy had visited this church, and reported some things that should be corrected, and that is one reason why the letter was written. They are commended for having become Christians and are exhorted to godliness. He comforts them relative to their dead friends and speaks of the second coming of Christ.

2 Thessalonians. By Paul. This letter was called forth by a reply to the first letter he had written them. In this he assures them of the great departure that would come before Christ would make his second advent.

1 Timothy. By Paul. Instructing Timothy, the young preacher, as to his work as an evangelist. The "setting in order" of congregations. Qualifications of elders and deacons.

2 Timothy. By Paul. Exhortation to constancy. Final charge to Timothy.

Titus. By Paul. Titus was a Gentile convert. The object of the letter was to instruct him in his duties as an evangelist.

Philemon. By Paul. Onesimus had been a servant of Philemon, and left him. Possibly he had not acted honorably with Philemon. Later he was converted by Paul and was sent by Paul with the letter to Philemon, requesting that he be received, as a brother.

Hebrews. Addressed to the Hebrews, who had been converted from the old religion. The entire burden of the letter is to show the superiority of the gospel over the law and the system of worship and blessings promised therein.

James. By James, a relative, possibly, a brother, of the Lord. He speaks at length of the character of faith that saves.

1 and 2 Peter. By Peter. Tells of our relationship to God. The relationship of husband and wife. Instruction to elders. Foretells of the rise of false teachers, the second coming of Christ and the destruction of the world.

1, 2 and 3 John. He discusses the life those who are Christians will live.

Jude. A denunciation of the false teachers.

Revelation. By John. The assurance of the final triumph of the gospel, and the final gathering of all God's people in the home of happiness.

CHAPTERS AND VERSES

The Bible was divided into chapters by Hugo in 1240.

Old Testament divided into verses by Mordecai Nathan in 1445.

New Testament divided into verses by Robert Steven in 1551.

HOW THE APOSTLES DIED

The following is the account generally given:

John: Died a natural death.

Matthew: Slain with a sword in Ethiopia.

James, son of Zebedee: Beheaded at Jerusalem.

James, brother of the Lord: Thrown from the pinnacle of the temple, then killed with a club.

Philip: Hanged against a pillar at Hieropolis, a city of Phrygia.

Bartholomew: Flayed alive at Albahapolis, in Armenia.

Andrew: Martyred on a cross at Patre, in Archaia.

Thomas: Killed with a lance at Coromanded, in East Indies.

Thaddeus: Shot to death with arrows.

Simon Zelotes: Crucified in Persia.

Peter: Crucified, head downward.

Matthias: Stoned, then beheaded.

Paul: Beheaded at Rome.

Judas: Hanged himself.

APOSTASY.

Man is a moral agent, before and after conversion. If man cannot fall after conversion, he is not free, but is no more than a machine.

Cannot—Not, Will Not.

Let me insist that you keep in mind the issue. It is not "will," but "can." It is not what a child of God "will do," but what they "can do." Can. Is it possible for one to become a child of God, and then to so act that he will be lost?

God No Respecter of Persons:

Acts 10:34. "Of a truth I perceive that God is no respecter of persons." "The soul that sinneth, it shall die." Ezek. 18:20.

Devil's Doctrine:

That a child of God cannot so act as to be lost, is the doctrine the devil taught in the Garden of Eden. "Ye shall not surely die." Gen. 3:4.

The Devil a Fool:

If a child of God cannot so far fall as to be finally lost, the devil is the biggest fool I ever heard of, for he has been trying for 6,000 years to get a child of God, and if he has not succeeded he is a fool for not quitting.

Are We More Secure than Angels?

2 Pet. 2:4. "God spared not the angels that sinned, but cast them down to hell, and delivered them into chains of darkness, to be reserved unto judgment."

Make Calling and Election Sure:

2 Pet. 1:10. "Brethren, give diligence to make your calling and election sure: for if ye do these things, ye shall never fall."

Take Heed Lest Ye Fall:

1 Cor. 10:12. "Wherefore let him that thinketh he standeth take heed lest he fall."

Keep Under Body:

1 Cor. 9:27. "But I keep under my body, and bring it into subjection: lest that by any means, when I have preached to others, I myself should be a castaway."

If Keep Sayings:

Jno. 8:51. "If a man keep my sayings, he shall never see death."

Live After the Flesh—Die:

Rom. 8:13. "For if ye live after the flesh, ye shall die: but if ye through the Spirit do mortify the deeds of the body, ye shall live."

Abide in. Remain in:

1 Jno. 2:24. "Let that therefore abide in you, which ye have heard from the beginning. If that which ye have heard from the beginning shall remain in you, ye also shall continue in the Son, and in the Father."

Wilful Sin:

Heb. 10:26. "For if we sin wilfully after that we have received the knowledge of the truth, there remaineth no more sacrifice for sin."

Was Sanctified. Does Despite to Spirit:

Heb. 10:29. "Of how much sorer punishment, suppose ye, shall he be thought worthy, who hath trodden under foot the Son of God, and hath counted the blood of the covenant, wherewith he was sanctified, an unholy thing, and hath done despite unto the Spirit of grace?"

Believers Condemned:

1 Cor. 11:29. "For he that eateth and drinketh unworthily, eateth and drinketh damnation to himself." The disbeliever is

"condemned already," Jno. 3:18, and could not eat and drink "damnation" to himself. If the child of God that eats and drinks "condemnation" will not—cannot—be lost, then why will the sinner that is "condemned" be lost? Are not God's ways equal?

Last State:

2 Peter 2:20, 21. "For if after they have escaped the pollutions of the world through the knowledge of the Lord and Saviour Jesus Christ, they are again entangled therein, and overcome, the latter end is worse with them than the beginning. For it had been better for them not to have known the way of righteousness than, after they have known it, to turn from the holy commandment delivered unto them." Note—(1) Escaped the pollutions of the world. (2) Entangled again therein. (3) Overcome. (4) Latter end worse than the beginning. (5) Better not to have known the way of righteousness, than (6), after they had known it, to (7) turn from the holy commandment.

In Kingdom—Gathered Out:

Jno. 3:5. "Except a man be born of water and of the Spirit, he cannot enter into the kingdom of God." It is positive: if a man is not born again, he *cannot* enter the kingdom. Then all in the kingdom have been born again, are children of God.

Gathered Out of Kingdom—Cast Into Fire:

Matt. 13:41. "The Son of man shall send forth his angels, and they shall gather out of his kingdom all things that offend, and them which do iniquity: and shall cast them into a furnace of fire: there shall be wailing and gnashing of teeth." They will gather out of the kingdom, but there are none in the kingdom, but those who have been born again; then some who have been born again—the ones that do iniquity—will be gathered out, and cast into a furnace of fire. The furnace of fire is hell. Rev. 19:20.

Utterly Forget You:

Jer. 23:39-40. "Therefore, behold, I, even I, will utterly forget you, and I will forsake you, and the city that I gave you and your fathers, and cast you out of my presence: and I will bring an everlasting reproach upon you, and a perpetual shame, which shall not be forgotten." (1) Utterly forget you. (2) Forsake you. (3) Cast you out of my presence. (4) Everlasting reproach on you. (5) Perpetual shame.

I Will Disinherit:

Num. 14:12. "I will smite them with pestilence, and disinherit them."

Will Not Clear the Guilty:

Num. 14:18. "The Lord is longsuffering, and of great mercy, forgiving iniquity and transgression, and by no means clearing the guilty."

Israel.

God's Children:

Deut. 14:1. "Ye are the children of the Lord your God." Deut. 7:6. "For thou art an holy people unto the Lord thy God."

Fell. Destroyed:

1 Cor. 10:1-10. "Moreover, brethren, I would not that ye should be ignorant, how that all our fathers were under the cloud, and all passed through the sea; and were all baptized unto Moses in the cloud and in the sea; and did all eat the same spiritual meat; and did all drink the same spiritual drink: for

17

they drank of that spiritual rock which followed them: and that rock was Christ. But with many of them God was not well pleased: for they were overthrown in the wilderness. Now these things were our examples, to the intent we should not lust after evil things, as they also lusted. Neither be ye idolaters, as were some of them; as it is written, The people sat down to eat and drink, and rose up to play. Neither let us commit fornication, as some of them committed, and fell in one day three and twenty thousand. Neither let us tempt Christ, as some of them also tempted, and were destroyed of serpents. Neither murmur ye, as some of them also murmured, and were destroyed of the destroyer." Note—(1) Baptized unto Moses. (2) Ate spiritual meat. (3) Drank spiritual drink —Christ. (4) Overthrown in wilderness. (5) Lusted after evil things. (6) Idolaters. (7) Committed fornication. (8) 23,000 fell in one day. (9) Tempted Christ. (10) Murmured.

How Some of Them Died:

Num. 25:8. "And he went after the man of Israel into the tent, and thrust both of them through, the man of Israel, and the woman through the belly." They were killed in the very act of fornication.

Fornicators Cannot Be Saved:

Gal. 5:19-21. "Now the works of the flesh are manifest, which are these: Adultery, fornication, . . . They which do such things shall not inherit the kingdom of God."

Forget God.

My People Have Forgotten Me:

Jer. 2:32. "Can a maid forget her ornaments, or a bride her attire? yet my people have forgotten me days without number."

Forget God—Cast Into Hell:

Ps. 9:17. "The wicked shall be turned into hell, and all the nations that forget God." (1) "My people have forgotten me." (2) Those that forget God shall be "cast into hell." (3) Are those that are cast into hell saved?

Book of Life.

God's Children Have Name There:

Phil. 4:13. "I entreat thee also, true yoke-fellow, help those women which labor with me in the gospel, with Clement also, and with other my fellow laborers, whose names are in the book of life."

Blotted Out of God's Book:

Ex. 32:33. "Whosoever hath sinned against me, him will I blot out of my book."

Not Written in Book—Cast Into Hell:

Rev. 20:15. "And whosoever was not found written in the book of life was cast into the lake of fire."

Depart From Faith.

1 Tim. 4:1-2. "Now the Spirit speaketh expressly, that in the latter times some shall depart from the faith, giving heed to seducing spirits, and doctrines of devils; speaking lies in hypocrisy; having their conscience seared with a hot iron." Note—(1) Depart from the faith. (2) Heed seducing spirits. (3) Heed doctrines of devils. (4) Speak lies in hypocrisy. (5) Conscience seared.

Faith.

Having Damnation: Cast Off Faith:

1 Tim. 5:12. "Having damnation, because they have cast off their first faith."

Overthrow Faith:

2 Tim. 2:18. "Who concerning the truth have erred, saying that the resurrection is passed already; and overthrow the faith of some."

Made Shipwreck of Faith:

1 Tim. 1:19. "Holding faith, and a good conscience; which some having put away concerning faith have made shipwreck."

Believe for Awhile:

Lk. 8:13. "For a while believe, and in time of temptation fall away."

Own Servant:

Matt. 25:14. "For the kingdom of heaven is as a man traveling into a far country, who called his own servants, and delivered unto them his goods." Of the number of his "own servants" he said there was an unprofitable one, which he directed to be

Cast Into Fire:

Matt. 25:30. "And cast ye the unprofitable servant into outer darkness: there shall be weeping and gnashing of teeth."

Vine and Branches:

Jno. 15:1-6. "I am the true vine, and my Father is the husbandman. Every branch in me that beareth not fruit is taken away. . . . If a man abide not in me, he is cast forth as a branch, and is withered; and men gether them, and cast them into the fire, and they are burned." Note—(1) Christ is the vine. (2) The branches are *in* him. (3) If a man abide not in him. (4) He is cast into the fire.

Left First Love:

Rev. 2:4-5. "Nevertheless I have somewhat against thee, because thou has left thy first love. Remember therefore from whence thou

20

art fallen, and repent, and do thy first works; or else I will come unto thee quickly, and will remove thy candlestick out of his place, except thou repent."

Turned Aside After Satan:

1 Tim. 5:15. "For some have already turned aside after Satan."

Fall From Grace:

Gal. 5:4. "Christ is become of no effect unto you, whosoever of you are justified by the law; ye are fallen from grace."

Fail of the Grace of God:

Heb. 12:14-15. "Follow peace with all men, and holiness, without which no man shall see the Lord: looking diligently lest any man fail [fall back from, R.V.] the grace of God."

Saul.

1 Sam. 10:6-10. "And the Spirit of the Lord will come upon thee, and thou shalt prophesy with them. . . . For God shall be with thee. . . . Seven days shalt thou tarry, till I come to thee, and show thee what thou shalt do. . . . And the Spirit of the Lord came upon him, and he prophesied among them." Note—(1) Spirit of Lord came upon him. (2) Prophesied. (3) God shall be with thee.

God Departs From; Becomes Enemy Of:

1 Sam. 28:16. "Then said Samuel, Wherefore then dost thou ask of me, seeing the Lord is departed from thee, and is become thine enemy?" Note—(1) God departs from Saul. (2) Becomes the enemy of Saul.

Saul Kills Himself:

1 Sam. 31:4-5. "Therefore Saul took a sword, and fell upon it. And when his armour

bearer saw that Saul was dead, . . ." Do those who are guilty of murder go to heaven?

Brother Perishes.

1 Cor. 8:11. "And through thy knowledge shall the weak brother perish, for whom Christ died." What does "perish" mean?

God's Way Equal.

The Way of the Lord is Equal:
Ezk. 33:17-19. "Yet the children of thy people say, The way of the Lord is not equal: but as for them, their way is not equal. When the righteous turneth from his righteousness, and committeth iniquity, he shall even die thereby. But if the wicked turneth from his wickedness, and do that which is lawful and right, he shall live thereby."

Keep Yourselves in the Love of God:
Jude 21. "Keep yourselves in the love of God."

Apostasy.

From the foregoing we learn that to be in harmony with God one must be in harmony with his will, *i.e.,* you are in harmony with God only when you conform to his will. It follows: When men cease to conform to the will of God, they cease to be in harmony with God. This is what is meant by "apostasy" or "falling from grace."

The above scriptures show people who were in harmony with God—in the favor of God, and some of them rejected the law of God, and as a result did not continue to enjoy his favor.

In the face of the above scriptures, some declare that you cannot fall from grace or apostatise.

22

As "grace" means "favor," if you "cannot fall from grace," then a child of God cannot so live as to cause the displeasure of God.

Can a child of God lie? You answer, "yes." Did he fall from the grace or favor of God, when he lied? If "no," then God favors lying. Do you ask why? Because, he did not fail of God's favor when he lied, if he did not fall from grace or favor. So it is with every sin. If a child of God can lie, what will the result be? "All liars shall have their part in the lake which burneth with fire and brimstone." Rev. 21:8. So certain as a child of God lies, and does not repent, he will be lost.

If a child of God cannot sin, and be lost, why did God give a law of pardon for his erring children?

You read: "He that heareth my word, and believeth on him that sent me, hath everlasting life, and shall not come into condemnation; but is passed from death unto life." Jno. 5:24. They "passed out of death." How were they dead? "Dead in trespasses and sins." (Eph. 2:1). Then life from that death is life from sin—it is pardon or forgiveness. One cannot live to God and live in sin. The "life" from sin, is "eternal life" from them. Sins once pardoned are never remembered against you. In this sense you have "eternal life," *i.e.,* you will not come into condemnation for those sins again.

As man became dead in sins by violating God's law, it follows that he will die a similar death every time he sins—violates God's law. If this is not true, then the same cause ceases to produce the same effect; in fact you will have a cause without an effect.

God says: "The soul that sinneth, it shall die." Ezk. 18:20. Die how? In sin. Hence, if a

23

child of God sins, he dies. What is the effect of this death? God says: "Your iniquities have separated between you and your God." Isa. 59:2. When the child of God sins, he is certainly separated from God.

Earnestly praying for the people of God, Solomon said: "If they sin against thee, (for there is no man that sinneth not) and thou be angry with them, and deliver them to the enemy . . . yet if they shall bethink themselves . . . and repent, and make supplications unto thee." 1 Ki. 8:46-47. Here we learn that God's people can, and did sin; and that he became angry with them; and that they must "repent, and make supplications" to be restored to the favor of God.

It is self evident that man cannot sin prior to his existence, for prior to his existence, he did not exist. You must exist before you can sin. This being true, every sin you commit must be while you exist. As there is no pardon for you after death, you must be pardoned of all your sins while you live; if you die in your sins, and Jesus says: "Whither I go, ye cannot come." Jno. 8:21. The man that dies in sin cannot be with Jesus in glory.

Pardon is confined to time, *i.e.*, you cannot be pardoned after you reach eternity. But as time is not eternity, and eternity is not time, why did Jesus say: "Hath everlasting life"? In the sense I have shown above, *viz.*, life, pardon, from death in sin. When God pardons, he remembers the sins no more; hence "everlasting life" from that death. When you sin again you pass into a state of condemnation, death. "The soul that sinneth, it shall die." That soul will remain in death till pardoned, and as there is no pardon beyond the grave, then you must be pardoned during your life here, or die in your sins, and to die in your sins, you cannot be with Jesus in eternity.

You can be saved from past sins, only, *i.e.*, sins of your past life; for you have not lived in the future, and you cannot sin during a time that has not existed. Future time has no existence. I mean, "tomorrow," as time, does not exist till you reach it, or till tomorrow comes. We have today, and live *now*, and not in the future; and for that reason all the sins you have had pardoned were sins of the past life. Sin must exist before it can be sin. When committed it is charged against you as a deed that is done, hence, past. I am fully persuaded that if you will study the above carefully you will see the necessity of getting right and remaining right, or be lost.

BAPTISM

Baptism Requires

Water:

Matt. 3:11. "I indeed baptize you with water." Sprinkling requires water.

Much Water:

Jno. 3:23. "And John was baptizing in Aenon near to Salim, because there was much water there." "Much water" is not necessary for sprinkling.

Go to Water:

Acts 8:36. "And as they went on their way, they came unto a certain water: and the eunuch said, See, here is water; what doeth hinder me to be baptized?" In sprinkling they usually bring the water—don't go to it.

Go Into Water:

Acts 8:38. "And he commanded the chariot to stand still: and they went down both into the water, both Philip and the eunuch; and he baptized him." In sprinkling they do not go "down into the water."

Burial:

Col. 2:12. "Buried with him in baptism." In sprinkling there is not a "burial."

Raised:

Rom. 6:4. "Therefore we are buried with him by baptism into death; that like as Christ was raised up from the dead by the glory of the Father, even so we also should walk in newness of life." No being "raised" where sprinkling is practiced.

Come Out of Water:

Acts 8:39. "And when they were come up out of the water." Such is not the case where sprinkling is practiced.

Administrator Handles the Subject:

Matt. 28:19. "Go ye therefore, and teach all nations, baptizing them." Where people have water sprinkled on them the administrator handles the element, not the subject.

Therefore we are buried wIth him
by baptisM into death: that like
as Christ was raised up froM the dead
by thE glory of the
FatheR, even so
we alSo should walk in
newness of lifE.— Rom. 6:4.

Why Be Baptized?

Christ Commanded It:

Matt. 28:19. "Go ye therefore, and teach all nations, baptizing them in the name of the

26

Father, and of the Son, and of the Holy Ghost."

Believe, Baptized Saved:

Mk. 16:16. "He that believeth and is baptized shall be saved."

Repent, Be Baptized, Remission of Sins:

Acts 2:38. "Repent, and be baptized every one of you in the name of Jesus Christ for the remission of sins."

Commanded:

Acts 10:48. "And he commanded them to be baptized in the name of the Lord."

Be Baptized, Wash Away Sins:

Acts 22:16. "And now why tarriest thou? arise, and be baptized, and wash away thy sins, calling on the name of the Lord."

Baptized Into Christ:

Rom. 6:3. "Know ye not, that so many of us as were baptized into Jesus Christ were baptized into his death."

In Christ We Are New Creatures:

2 Cor. 5:17. "If any man be in Christ, he is a new creature." Note—(1) If we are in Christ, we are "new creatures." (2) We are "baptized into Christ." Gal. 3:27.

Redemption is in Christ:

Col. 1:14. "In whom we have redemption through his blood, even the forgiveness of sins."

Baptized Into Christ:

Gal. 3:27. "For as many of you as have been baptized into Christ have put on Christ." Note—(1) Redemption is in Christ. (2) We are "baptized into Christ."

Baptism Saves:

1 Pet. 3:21. "The like figure whereunto even baptism doth also now save us."

Then Peter said unto them Re**P**ent and be baptized every one
of you in the n**A**me of Jesus Christ
for the **R**emission of sins
an**D** ye shall receive the gift
of the Holy Gh**O**st. For the promise is to you
and to your childre**N**. — Acts 2:38.

*When Baptism and Salvation are Mentioned
in the Same Passage, Salvation is Always
Mentioned After Baptism:*

Mk. 1:4. "John did baptize in the wilderness, and preach the baptism of repentance for remission of sins."

Baptism, Remission of Sins:

Lk. 3:3. "Preaching the baptism of repentance for the remission of sins."

Baptized, Saved:

Mk. 16:16. "He that believeth and is baptized shall be saved."

Baptized, Remission of Sins:

Acts 2:38. "Repent, and be baptized every one of you in the name of Jesus Christ for the remission of sins."

Baptized, Wash Away Sins:

Acts 22:16. "Arise, and be baptized, and wash away thy sins."

Baptized, Sins:

1 Pet. 3:21. "Baptism doth also now save us."

In Christ.

If in Christ—New Creature:

2 Cor. 5:17. "If any man be in Christ, he is a new creature: old things are passed away; behold all things are become new."

Redemption in Christ:

Col. 1:13-14. "Who hath delivered us from the power of darkness, and hath translated us into the kingdom of his dear Son: in whom we have redemption through his blood, even the forgiveness of sins.''

Promises Are in Christ:

2 Cor. 1:20. "For all the promises of God in him are yea, and in him Amen."

Baptized Into Christ:

Gal. 3:27. "For as many of you as have been baptized into Christ have put on Christ."

Baptized Into Christ:

Rom. 6:3. "Know ye not, that so many of us as were baptized into Jesus Christ were baptized into his death."

Note—In Christ we are "new creatures," "redemption" is "in Christ." We are "baptized into Christ" where the "redemption" is—where we are "new creatures."

Who Were Baptized—Were Infants?

Jesus came aNd spake unto them
saying, All pOwer is given unto me in
heaven and in earTh. Go ye therefore

and teach all nAtions,
baptiziNg them

In the
Name of the
Father,
And of the Son,
aNd of the
Holy GhosT.—Matt. 28:18-19.

Confessed Sins:

Mk. 1:5. "And there went out unto him all the land of Judea, and they of Jerusalem, and were all baptized of him in the river of Jordan, confessing their sin." Do infants "confess sins"?

29

Made and Baptized Disciples:

Jno. 4:1. "When therefore the Lord knew how the Pharisees had heard that Jesus made and baptized more disciples than John, though Jesus himself baptized not, but his disciples." Are infants "disciples"?

Teach and Baptize:

Matt. 28:19. "Go ye therefore and teach all nations, baptizing them. Do you "teach infants"?

Received Word—Baptized:

Acts 2:41. "Then they that gladly received his word were baptized." Do infants "receive his word gladly"?

Repent and Be Baptized:

Acts 2:38. "Repent, and be baptized every one of you in the name of Jesus Christ for the remission of sins." Do infants "repent"?

Men and Women:

Acts 8:12. "But when they believed Philip preaching the things concerning the kingdom of God, and the name of Jesus Christ, they were baptized, both men and women." Not an infant in that number!

Believed—Baptized:

Acts 8:38. "And he commanded the chariot to stand still: and they went down both into the water, both Philip and the eunuch; and he baptized him." No infants there.

Saul of Tarsus:

Acts 9:18. "And immediately there fell from his eyes as it had been scales: and he received his sight forthwith, and arose, and was baptized."

Cornelius:

Acts 10:48. "And he commanded them to be baptized."

Lydia and Her Household:

Acts 16:15. "And when she was baptized, and her household, she besought us, saying, If ye have judged me to be faithful to the Lord, come into my house, and abide there. And she constrained us." Were there infants in that household? Let's see. Verse 40: "And they [Paul and Silas] went out of the prison, and entered into the house of Lydia: and when they had seen the brethren, they comforted them, and departed." "Comforted them." Were Paul and Silas "comforting" infants?

Heard, Believed, and Were Baptized:

Acts 18:8. "And Crispus, the chief ruler of the synagogue, believed on the Lord with all his house; and many of the Corinthians hearing, believed and were baptized." Not an infant in that number.

Twelve Men at Ephesus:

Acts 19:8.

Answer of a Good Conscience:

1 Pet. 3:19-21. "By which also he went and preached unto the spirits in prison; which sometime were disobedient, when once the longsuffering of God waited in the days of Noah, while the ark was a preparing, wherein few, that is, eight souls were saved by water. The like figure whereunto even baptism doth also now save us (not the putting away of the filth of the flesh, but the answer of a good conscience towards God), by the resurrection of Jesus Christ." How can an unconscious infant have a "good conscience"?

In all the cases of baptism mentioned in the word of God there is not the mention of an infant.

31

Jesus came aNd spake unto them,
saying, all pOwer is given unto me

in Heaven and In earth. Go ye therefore,
and teach all Nations, baptizing them in
the name of theFather,
        And of the Son,
      aNd of the
Holy GhosT. —Matt. 28:18-19.

Baptism.

I have cited the above scriptures to show:

1. What baptism requires.
2. Why be baptized.
3. Who were baptized—were infants?

There is no controversy over "immersion" of a proper subject, being baptism. Comment on that point is not necessary. The above scriptures are sufficient for all who are willing to accept the Bible.

Is "sprinkling or pouring water on a proper subject baptism?" As baptizing is something done—an act performed, if "sprinkle," "pour" and "immerse," as distinct acts, are all baptizing, then we have three distinct acts that are equal to the same thing—or same act—baptize.

"Sprinkle" is not "pour," nor is "pour" sprinkle, and neither of these acts are equivalent to the act "immerse." If the act "sprinkle" is equal to the act "baptize," and the act "pour" differs from the act "sprinkle," could the act pour be equal to the act "baptize"? Since the act "immerse" differs from both the act "sprinkle" and "pour," can the act "immerse" equal "baptize" too?

If "immersing" is baptism, and all say it is; since "sprinkling" or "pouring" water on a person, differs from the act "immerse,"

32

how in the name of reason can one call it by the same name? "Immersion" is baptism; but "sprinkling" or "pouring" water on a person differs from the act "immerse" and therefore cannot be the same thing!

The advocates of "sprinkling" and "pouring" for baptism refer to the sprinklings under the law of Moses, and declare they were baptisms. The word "sprinkle" was never used by an inspired man to convey the idea of baptizing. Many teach otherwise, hence the necessity of showing the fallacy of such a contention.

Paul preached and baptized people. He says: "But I certify you, brethren, that the gospel which was preached of me is not after men. For I neither received it of man, neither was I taught it, but by the revelation of Jesus Christ." Gal. 1:11-12. Hear him again: "I am verily a man which am a Jew, born in Tarsus, a city in Cilicia, yet brought up in this city at the feet of Gamaliel, and taught according to the perfect manner of the law of the fathers." Acts 22:3. Note: Paul was taught the law by Gamaliel—a man; but he says: "The gospel which was preached of me is not after man. For I neither received it of man, neither was I taught it, but by the revelation of Jesus Christ." Though he was taught the "law" by Gamaliel, the gospel which he preached was not taught him by man. The "law," contained the sprinklings and pourings referred to by paedo-baptists, and called by them baptism. Paul was taught the "law" by man, but the gospel he preached was not taught him by man. As Paul knew the law, being taught it by Gamaliel, but did not know the Gospel till it was revealed to him by Christ, it follows that the

33

"law" is not the gospel, nor can the sprinklings of the law be the "baptism" that Paul preached, nor can the "baptism" he preached be the sprinklings of the law.

"By the deeds of the law there shall no flesh be justified." Rom. 3:20. If you take "sprinkling" for baptism, you take a deed of the law, and God says you cannot be justified by such. Not only so, but Moses would be the author of your baptism, and your baptism would be neither "grace" nor "truth," for the "law was given by Moses, but grace and truth came by Jesus Christ." Jno. 1:17. "Grace and truth" came by Christ, as contrasted with the law which came by Moses.

The things Paul preached were revealed to him "by the Spirit." 1 Cor. 2:10-13. He did not preach till some years after Christ went to glory. It follows then that it was after Christ ascended that the baptism Paul preached was revealed to him. But Paul had been acquainted with the law and the sprinklings of the law all his life. It follows, by all force of logic and scripture, that the baptism Paul preached was not the sprinklings of the law.

Would you have additional proof? Here it is: Paul preached "the faith which once he destroyed." Gal. 1:23. But Paul preached the gospel. 1 Cor. 15:1. It follows then that to preach "the faith" is to preach "the gospel." Concluding this thought: Paul says: "But before faith came, we were kept under the law, shut up unto the faith which should afterwards be revealed." Col. 3:23. Remember, Paul says the gospel he preached was revealed unto him by the Spirit, and that this revelation was since the law. That which Paul preached was revealed unto him after the

34

law. If "sprinkling" was baptism, it was revealed in the law, and hence could not have been since the law. It follows then: the baptism of the gospel is different from anything in the law.

Briefly: What Is Baptism For?

"If any man be in Christ, he is a new creature." 2 Cor. 5:17. Again: "That they may obtain the salvation which is in Christ." 2 Tim. 2:10. You must be "in Christ" to be a "new creature." "Salvation" is "in Christ." The word of God says: "For as many of you as have been baptized into Christ have put on Christ." Gal. 3:27. Salvation is in Christ; we are baptized into Christ where we receive the salvation.

Is baptism a command of the gospel? If you say "no"; then since a man cannot get into a church without baptism, it follows that the gospel of Christ will not put a man into a church. As the gospel is the "power of God," if baptism is no part of the "power of God," and as you get into the church by baptism, you do not get into the church by the "power of God." If man gets into the church by the power of God, and comes in by baptism, then baptism belongs to the power of God.

Again: If you are saved without baptism, you are saved without the power of God, for baptism is in the gospel, and the gospel is the power of God.

Christ Sent Me Not To Baptize.

Those who teach that baptism is not a condition of salvation often contend that Paul was not sent to baptize, because of the following passage:

Christ Sent Me Not to Baptize:

1 Cor. 1:17. "For Christ sent me not to baptize, but to preach the gospel."

It is a fact that Paul baptized some people, for he declared, "I baptized none of you but Crispus and Gaius; . . . I baptized also the household of Stephanus." 1 Cor. 1:14-16. Will anyone contend that when Paul baptized these people he did something he was not sent to do?

When Christ gave the Great Commission he certainly commanded that believers be baptized. "Go ye therefore, and teach all nations, baptizing them." If Paul labored under the same commission as the other apostles, he was commanded to baptize the believers.

Paul Was Faithful:

2 Tim. 4:7. "I have fought a good fight. I have finished my course, I have kept the faith." Since Paul was faithful, it must follow that when he baptized believers, Crispus, Gaius and others, he was doing what the Lord commanded.

Believe Not On Me:

Jno. 12:44. "Jesus cried and said, He that believeth on me, believeth not on me, but on him that sent me."

Do you believe on Jesus? Certainly you do. But Jesus says, "He that believeth on me, believeth not on me." Surely every one understands that the passage is elliptical, and to supply the ellipsis it reads: He that believeth on me, believeth not on me [only], but [also] on him that sent me. Everyone knows this to be true. One cannot believe on Jesus without believing on God.

36

Sent Me Not to Baptize:

1 Cor. 1:14. "Christ sent me not to baptize, but to preach the gospel."

But Paul did baptize, and, too, he was faithful.

This passage must be elliptical, and if we supply the ellipsis, it will read: Christ sent me not to baptize [only], but [also] to preach the gospel.

Jno. 12:44. "He that believeth on me, believeth not on me [only], but [also] on him that sent me."

1 Cor. 1:14. "Christ sent me not to baptize [only] but [also] to preach the gospel."

And, too, anyone could baptize, but only an inspired man could preach (reveal) the gospel, then.

Paul reached Corinth before his helpers (Silas and Timothy). (See Acts 18:1-5). As the family of Stephanas was the first fruits (converts) in Corinth (1 Cor. 16:15), it is evident those Paul baptized were converted before his helpers arrived. With Paul baptism was so important that he did not neglect it; hence, in the absence of his helpers he administered the baptism himself. When all the circumstances are considered, we see the importance Paul attached to baptism.

Because some were calling themselves after the name of men, Paul was glad that circumstances had not made it necessary for him to baptize others. He inquires: "Were ye baptized in the name of Paul?" He by this teaches that one has no right to wear the name of one into whose name they have not been baptized. You have no right to wear the name of Christ till you have been baptized into his name.

37

All the Corinthians that believed were baptized. Acts 18:8.

WATER

For Water.

God.
   The Flood. Gen. 7
   Red Sea. Ex. 14.
Christ.
   Born of Water. Jno. 3.
   Baptized. Matt. 3.
Heaven.
   Baptism of John. Matt. 21:25.
   River of Life. Rev. 22:1.
John.
   Much Water. Jno. 3:23.
   In Jordan. Matt. 3:6.
Peter.
   Who can forbid water? Acts 10:48.

Against Water.

The Devil.
   Defeats: Pharaoh. Ex. 14.
   Swine. Matt. 8:32.
Evil Spirits.
   Walks through dry places. Matt. 12:43.
Hell.
   Quenches fire. Lk. 16.
   Dry country.

There are people today that are opposed to water when it comes to matters that pertain to religion. On which side are you?

————

ONE BODY

One Body:
Rom. 12:4-5. "For as we have many members in one body, and all members have not the same office: so we, being many, are one body in Christ."

One Body:
1 Cor. 12:12. "For as the body is one, and hath many members, and all the members of that one body, being many are one body, so also is Christ."

One Body:
Eph. 2:16. "That he might reconcile both unto God in one body by the cross, having slain the enmity thereby."

One Body:
Col. 3:15. "Let the peace of God rule in your hearts, to which also ye are called in one body."

One Body:
Eph. 4:4. "There is one body."

What Is The One Body?

The Body—the Church:
Col. 1:18. "And he is the head of the body, the church."

The Church Which Is His Body:
Eph. 1:22-23. "And gave him to be head over all things to the church, which is his body."

The Body—Which Is the Church:
Col. 1:24. "For his body's sake, which is the church."

Head of Church—The Body.

Christ:
Col. 1:18. "And he is the head of the body, the church."

Christ:

Eph. 1:22. "And gave him to be head over all things to the church."

Christ:

Eph. 5:23. "For the husband is the head of the wife, even as Christ is the head of the church."

Must We Be Members of the "One Body" —The Church—To Be Saved?

Saviour of the Body:

Eph. 5:23. "For the husband is the head of the wife, even as Christ is the head of the church: and he is the saviour of the body."

Gave Himself for Church:

Eph. 5:25. "Husbands, love your wives, even as Christ also loved the church, and gave himself for it."

Purchased the Church with His Blood:

Acts 20:28. "Feed the church of God, which he hath purchased with his own blood."

Reconciled in the One Body:

Eph. 2:16. "That he might reconcile both unto God in one body."

Added to Church:

Acts 2:47. "And the Lord added to the church daily such as should be saved."

Since the "church" is the "body" and Christ is the "saviour of the body," how can men be saved and not be members of the church? Again. Since he "purchased" the church with his own blood, how can people be saved and not be members of the purchased institution?

The church is spoken of as God's family— God's household.

"For this cause I bow my knees unto the Father of our Lord Jesus Christ, of whom the

whole family in heaven and earth is named."
Eph. 3:14-15. Again: "But if I tarry long,
that thou mayest know how thou oughtest to
behave thyself in the house of the living God,
which is the church of the living God." 1 Tim. 3:15.
From these scriptures we learn that the
church is God's family—God's household. If
people are saved before they are members of
the church, then it runs thus: If you are
saved, if you are a child of God, but not a
member of the church: then you are a child
but not in the family. If you are a child, and
not in the family (church), you accuse God of
being the father of children that are not in his
family! Again: You had to be "born again" to
be saved: If you are saved before you become
a member of the church, since the church is
God's family; it follows that you were born
again, and remained out of the family of God.
Why? 1st. You had to be born again to be
saved. 2nd. When saved, you are God's child,
or when born again, you are God's child. If
saved before you became one of God's
family—the church—then you claim to be a
child and not in the family of God. I would
hate to accuse God of having children that
are not in his family, and I would certainly
hate to acknowledge that I was a child of
God and not in his family. God does not have
children who are not in his family, and the
family is the church. It follows that all God's
children are members of his family—the
church.

Use the Word "Church."

The word "church" sometimes has
reference to a local congregation of Christians who have met for worship; and sometimes it is used to designate all of God's

41

children on earth, with no reference to geographical location.

In a General Sense.

Matt. 16:18. "Upon this rock I will build my church."

Col. 1:18. "And he is the head of the body, the church.

Eph. 1:22. "And gave him to be the head over all things to the church."

Eph. 5:25. "Husbands, love your wives, even as Christ also loved the church, and gave himself for it."

In a Local Sense.

1 Cor. 1:2. "Unto the church of God which is at Corinth."

1 Cor. 16:19. "Aquila and Priscilla salute you much in the Lord, with the church that is in their house."

Philemon 2. "To the church in thy house."

The word "churches" (plural), in the scripture is never used to designate different kinds of institutions. Where you find the plural, churches, reference is made to the church in different places, as the church at Rome, Corinth, Ephesus, Sardis, Jerusalem. They were not different kinds of churches, but the one church at different places. Christians live at many places. When the Christians at any place assemble for worship, that is the church at that place, and are a part of the church, when reference is made to the church in the general sense. Christ is the one head of the church. In the local congregations bishops are appointed to guide or teach, as directed by Christ, the chief Shepherd.

You cannot have government without law, nor different kinds of governments without different laws. Things that differ cannot harmonize—till the things causing the differences are set aside. People that are guided by the word of God cannot differ, for the law of God cannot differ from itself. The only way we can possibly have different churches, is to have different laws; for the church of Christ is a people guided by the law of God. If a people take the laws, rules and regulations of men, they are a human institution, purely so. The nature of every institution is determined by the nature of the law they are governed by. If the law is divine, then the institution will be a divine one. As the church or kingdom of God are people governed by the law of God, they cannot differ, for the divine cannot differ from itself. A people observing the laws of man or governed by human law, cannot possibly claim, rightfully, to be a divine institution. The church of Christ is a divine institution. It must follow those who are governed by human law have no right to claim to be more than a human institution, and is no part of the church of Christ, the divine institution. Divine law and human law differ just as God differs from man. God's divine institution, the church, differs from human institutions, called churches, just as the human differs from the divine. If you are in a church you cannot read about in the Bible, you are in an institution that differs from the divine one. There is but one thing that can differ from the divine—that is the human institution. Are you a member of the divine institution?

Church.

Church of God:

1 Cor. 1:1-2. "Paul, called to be an apostle of Jesus Christ, through the will of God, and

43

Sosthenes our brother, unto the church of God which is at Corinth."

Church of God:

Acts 20:28. "Feed the church of God, which he hath purchased with his own blood."

My Church:

Matt. 16:17-18. "Jesus answered and said unto him, Blessed art thou, Simon Barjona: for flesh and blood hath not revealed it unto thee, but my Father which is in heaven. And I say also unto thee, That thou art Peter, and upon this rock I will build my church."

Churches of Christ:

Rom. 16:16. "The churches of Christ salute you."

Church of the Firstborn:

Heb. 12:23. "To the general assembly and church of the firstborn."

The Church—Its Membership.

Fear On All the Church:

Acts 5:11. "And great fear came upon all the church, and upon as many as heard these things." Were there infants in that church?

All Know the Lord:

Heb. 8:11. "And they shall not teach every man his neighbor, and every man his brother, saying, Know the Lord: for all shall know me, from the least to the greatest." Not an infant in the number.

Same Care for Each Other:

1 Cor. 12:25. "That there should be no schism in the body; but that the members should have the same care one for another." Do you think there were infants in that membership?

Edified Itself:

Eph. 4:16. "From which the whole body fitly joined together and compacted by that which every joint supplieth, according to the effectual working in the measure of every part, maketh increase of the body unto the edifying of itself in love." Could infants edify?

Please the Whole Church:

Acts 15:22. "Then pleased it the apostles and elders, with the whole church, to send chosen men of their own company to Antioch with Paul and Barnabas." Infants do not send people.

Tell It to the Church:

Matt. 18:17. "And if he shall neglect to hear them, tell it unto the church." You know there was not an infant in that number.

Went Everywhere Preaching:

Acts 8:3-4. "As for Saul, he made havoc of the church, entering into every house, and hailing men and women, committed them to prison. Therefore they that were scattered abroad went everywhere preaching the word."

There was not an infant in the church in the days of the apostles.

Body—Reconciled In.

Be Reconciled to God:

2 Cor. 5:20. "Now then we are ambassadors for Christ, as though God did beseech you by us: we pray you in Christ's stead, be ye reconciled to God."

Reconciled in the One Body:

Eph. 2:16. "And that he might reconcile both unto God in one body by the cross."

What Is the Body?

Col. 1:18. "And he is the head of the body, the church."

Since we are "reconciled" in the body, and the "body" is the church, then reconciliation is in the church. But all people teach that we are baptized into the church; then do they not teach that baptism is necessary to reconciliation?

When I speak of the "church of Christ" in its generic sense, I have reference to heaven's ordained institution. When I speak of the "church of God," I mean all God's people on earth, over whom Christ reigns supremely. I do not mean that the church is an invisible, mystical nothing that people get into. I mean, the church is the people, the children of God, and the children of God are the church of God. I want you to understand that the children of God are "members one of another," and thus constitute the entire family. In becoming a member of the church you comply with the law necessary to salvation; and when saved, you are one of the number of the saved, by reason of being saved.

I insist that if one can be saved without being a member of the church, by reason of being saved, then all men can be saved, and none of them be a member of the church, or bear any relationship to it. But if all can be saved and not be members of the church, I would like for someone to tell: Who will constitute the church? One cannot be saved without being one of the number of the saved. It takes all the saved to constitute the saved number; then all the saved are numbered together. All the saved are numbered together; but if they can be saved without

46

being in the church, who are members of the church?

Paul says: "For as we have many members in one body, and all members have not the same office: so we, being many, are one body in Christ, and every one members one of another." Rom. 12:4-5. Again: "And hath put all things under his feet, and gave him to be head over all things to the church, which is his body, the fullness of him that filleth all in all." Eph. 1:22-23. Here we learn that Christians constitute the body of Christ. Though there are "many members," there is but one body—that all are "members one of another;" and that it takes all the saved to constitute this number. You should remember: there is only one church, and Christ is the head. Though the church is composed of many members, they are all "in Christ;"—"In whom [Christ] all the building fitly framed together groweth unto an holy temple in the Lord: in whom ye also are builded together for an habitation of God through the Spirit." Eph. 2:21-22. The building—church—is said to be framed together, and thus framed, they are said to grow unto a holy temple of God. Writing to the brethren at Corinth, they are called the "temple of God." 1 Cor. 3:16.

The church is the body of Christ. If you are not a member of the church—one of the number constituting the church, you are no part of the body of Christ. To be in Christ is to be in his body—the church. Then to fail to be in his body—the church—is to be out of Christ. Speaking of Christ, John says: "In him was life, and the life was the light of men." Jno. 1:4. As the life is in him, and the life is the light of men; if you are not in him, you are not where life is, neither are you in the light. But to be in him is to be in his body —the church—"and gave him to be head over all things to the church, which is his body, the fullness of him that filleth all in all." Eph. 1:22-23.

The church is the body of Christ, the saved are members of that body. The circulation of the body is necessary to the life of each member of the body. If you have no connection with the body, you do not have the life eminating from the body. Sever a member from the body and it cannot live, for the life of the member is dependent on connection with, and the circulation of the body. It is not possible for you to have connection with the body and not have membership in the body. As Christian life is the life of the body, and the body is the church of Christ, since you cannot have the life of the body separated from the body, then you cannot have Christian life separated from the body (church) of Christ.

To the church at Ephesus, Paul says: "Wherefore remember, that ye being in time past Gentiles in the flesh . . . that at that time ye were without Christ, . . . having no hope, and without God in the world: but now in Christ Jesus ye who sometimes were far off are made nigh by the blood of Christ." Eph. 2:11-13. Note: They were "far off; without Christ; without God or hope in the world;" but now "in Christ ye are . . . made nigh by the blood of Christ."

Since they were blessed "in Christ," it might be well to learn just what is meant by being "in Christ." Eph. 2:13. "For through him [being now in him, vs. 13] we both have access by one Spirit unto the Father." Vs.

48

18. Being in him, "ye are no more strangers and foreigners, but fellow citizens with the saints, and of the household of God." Vs. 19. Note, carefully: 1. They were "strangers and foreigners" till they came into the church. 2. When they came into the church, they ceased to be "strangers and foreigners," and became "citizens with the saints,"—(then all the saints were citizens). 3. But in becoming "citizens" they became members of the "household of God." The "house of God" is the church of God. 1 Tim. 3:15. They were without Christ, God, hope, strangers, foreigners till they came into Christ.

Now in Christ, they are citizens with the saints and of the household (church) of God. They had to be "in Christ" to be saved. If they were saved before they were in the church—the body of Christ—they were: 1. Not citizens. 2. They were not with the saints. 3. They were not upon the foundation of the apostles and prophets, nor in Christ the chief corner stone.

Born of God.

Whosoever Believeth:

1 Jno. 5:1. "Whosoever believeth that Jesus is the Christ is born of God."

Whosoever Loveth:

1 Jno. 4:7. "Every one that loveth is born of God."

Whosoever Doeth Righteousness:

1 Jno. 2:29. "Every one that doeth righteousness is born of him."

From the above it must follow that the one who "believeth," "loveth" and "doeth righteousness" is "born of God;" but, "all thy commandments are righteousness." Ps. 119:

49

172. Then the one who does the commandments of God is born of God.

Born of God and Knows God:

1 Jno. 4:7. "Every one that loveth is born of God and knoweth God."

What Is the Love of God:

1 Jno. 5:3. "For this is the love of God, that we keep his commandments."

Who Knows God:

1 Jno. 2:4. "He that saith, I know him, and keepeth not his commandments, is a liar, and the truth is not in him."

A few thoughts in connection with the above scriptures:

"He came unto his own, and his own received him not. But as many as received him, to them gave he power to become the sons of God, even to them that believe on his name: which were born, not of blood, nor of the will of the flesh, nor of the will of man, but of God"—*i.e.,* of the will of God. Jno. 1:11-13.

Again: "Except a man be born again . . . born of water and of the Spirit, he cannot enter into the kingdom of God." Jno. 3:3-5. Entrance into the kingdom of God is contingent on the new birth. This being true, it is necessary that you understand how this birth is brought about.

Jesus says: "Seek ye first the kingdom of God." Matt. 6:33. Again: "Not every one that saith unto me, Lord, Lord, shall enter into the kingdom of heaven; but he that doeth the will of my Father which is in heaven." Matt. 7:21.

Note: 1. You must be born again. 2. By this birth you enter the kingdom. 3. You seek the kingdom. 4. Must do will of God to enter the kingdom.

It stands thus: 1st. Born again, enter the kingdom, or 2nd. Do will of God, enter the kingdom. Then I must do the will of God to enter the kingdom, and when I do the will of God I am born again. It follows, then, that to "seek the kingdom" is to seek to know and do the will of God. When I do the will of God, I enter the kingdom; but I had to be born again to enter the kingdom; therefore when I do the will of God I am born again. One must be born again to be saved. Those born again are saved; but the saved are in Christ. It follows that whatever is necessary to bring one into Christ is necessary to the new birth, or the one that enters Christ does so by birth. Why? Because, (1) The one born again is saved. (2) Salvation is in Christ. (3) Therefore the birth brings into Christ. (4) You are baptized into Christ. Gal. 3:27. (5) Then in being baptized you are doing the will of God, and baptism is necessary to being born again.

To be in the kingdom, or church, is to be in Christ, for the church is the body of Christ; hence the birth is necessary to coming into the body—church—Christ. Since we are "baptized into Christ," it follows that baptism is necessary to the new birth—necessary to being born of God.

Peter says: "Of a truth, I perceive that God is no respecter of persons; but in every nation he that feareth him, and worketh righteousness, is accepted with him." Acts 10:34-35. Again: "If ye know that he is righteous, ye know that every one that doeth righteousness is born of him." 1 Jno. 2:29. Peter says that God accepts the man that doeth righteousness. John says the man that doeth righteousness is born of God. It follows one must be "born of him" before he will accept him. God "accepts" only those in Christ. Col. 1:14; Eph. 1:7. Therefore the birth brings into Christ, and as man is baptized into Christ, it follows that baptism is necessary to the birth. Man must do righteousness to be "accepted with him"—God—and the man that doeth righteousness is "born of him," then man must be born by doing righteousness, before God will accept him.

The righteousness of God is in the gospel. Rom. 1:17. David says the commandments of God are righteousness. Ps. 119:172. Then man must do the commandments of the gospel to be accepted of him. Righteousness is in the gospel, and is the commandments of God. man must do righteousness to be born of him. But baptism is one of the commands of the gospel. Therefore man must be baptized to be born of God.

"Seeing ye have purified your souls in obeying the truth." 1 Pet. 1:22.

1. Obedience to the truth purifies the soul. 2. Those who have pure souls are in Christ. 3. Therefore obedience to the truth brings into Christ. 4. The one who obeys the truth is born again. 5. The one who obeys the truth is saved. 6. Therefore the one who is born again is saved. 7. We are saved in Christ. 8. The one that is born again is saved. 9. Therefore the birth brings into Christ. 10. But man is baptized into Christ. 11. Therefore in being born again you must be baptized.

Peter says we are born of (in obedience to) incorruptible seed, "by the word of God . . .

and this is the word which by the gospel is preached unto you." 1 Pet. 1:22-25. When they obeyed the gospel, they obeyed the truth; when they obeyed the truth, they were saved; but they were saved in Christ; therefore obedience to the gospel brought them into Christ.

1. When they obeyed the truth, they were born again. 2. When they obeyed the truth, they were saved. 3. But they were saved in Christ. 4. We are baptized into Christ. 5. Therefore baptism is necessary to obedience to the truth—to the new birth.

HAS THE KINGDOM BEEN ESTABLISHED?

Christ Is King of Kings.

Rev. 17:14. "These shall make war with the Lamb, and the Lamb shall overcome them: for he is Lord of lords, and King of kings."

Lord's Table Is in Kingdom:

Lk. 22:30. "That ye may eat and drink at my table in my kingdom."

We Have the Lord's Table:

1 Cor. 10:21. "Ye cannot be partakers of the Lord's table, and the table of devils." Note—(1) The Lord's table was to be in the kingdom. (2) The brethren at Corinth had the Lord's table. (3) Therefore the kingdom was there.

Translated Into the Kingdom:

Col. 1:13. "Who hath delivered us from the power of darkness, and hath translated us into the kingdom of his dear Son."

In the Kingdom:

Rev. 1:9. "I, John, who also am your brother and companion in tribulation, and in the kingdom and patience of Jesus Christ."

Though Paul says the brethren at Colosse had been "translated into the kingdom," some declare that the kingdom does not exist, and will not be established till Christ comes at the end of this dispensation—at his second coming. If such be true, then the establishing of the kingdom and the second coming of Christ will be at the same time.

While on earth Christ said: "The kingdom of God is at hand." Mk. 1:15. It must follow, then, since the kingdom was "at hand," if the kingdom will not be established till the second coming of Christ, the second coming of Christ was also "at hand." But was the second coming of Christ "at hand" while Christ was on earth?

Paul declared some twenty-five years after the death of Christ that the second coming of Christ was *not* "at hand." Hear him: "Now I beseech you, brethren, by the coming of our Lord, Jesus Christ, and our gathering together unto him, that ye be not soon shaken in mind, or be troubled, neither by spirit, nor by word, nor by letter as from us, as that the day of Christ is at hand." 2 Thess. 2:1-2. In this Paul positively declares that the "day of Christ" was *not* "at hand." When is the "day of Christ?" It is the last day—the day of his coming the second time. "But the day of the Lord will come as a thief in the night; in the which the heavens shall pass away with a great noise, and the elements shall melt with fervent heat, the earth also and the works that are therein shall be burned up." 2 Pet. 3:10. This settles the matter that the "day of Christ" will be at the end of this world. Jesus declared, while he was on earth: "The kingdom of God is *at hand,*" and some 25 years afterwards Paul declared the second coming of Christ was *not "at hand."* If you believe what Paul and Christ have said, you cannot believe that the establishment of the kingdom and the second coming of Christ will be at the same time; for if the establishment of the kingdom and the second coming of Christ are to be at the same time, then they would have been equally near —"at hand"—when Christ was here. But Christ declared the kingdom was "at hand" and that his second coming would be "after a long time." Matt. 25:19.

(For a full discussion of this subject, see the *Nichol-Bradley Debate.*)

Church or Kingdom: When Established?

At Hand:

Matt. 3:2. "In those days came John the Baptist, preaching in the wilderness of Judea, and saying, Repent ye; for the kingdom of heaven is at hand."

At Hand:

Matt. 4:17. "From that time Jesus began to preach, and to say, Repent: for the kingdom of heaven is at hand."

After Christ Ordained the Twelve Apostles, He Said to Them:

Matt. 10:7. "Go preach, saying, The kingdom of heaven is at hand."

If the "kingdom of heaven is at hand" meant it was established when Christ told the twelve to preach such, why does not "kingdom of heaven is at hand" mean that it was established when John the Baptist preached it?

Is Come Nigh:

Lk. 10:9. "The kingdom of God is come nigh unto you."

To the Disciples Christ Said: Seek Ye the Kingdom of God:

Lk. 12:31. "But rather seek ye the kingdom of God."

To the Disciples Christ Promised the Kingdom:

Lk. 12:32. "Fear not, little flock; for it is your Father's good pleasure to give you the kingdom."

Will Build the Church:

Matt. 16:18. "And I say also unto thee, that thou art Peter, and upon this rock I will build my church; and the gates of hell shall not prevail against it."

Disciples Were Not in the Kingdom:

Matt. 18:3. "Verily I say unto you, Except ye be converted, and become as little children, ye shall not enter the kingdom of heaven."

Priests and Elders Not in Kingdom:

Matt. 21:31. "Verily I say unto you, that the publicans and harlots go into the kingdom of God before you."

Scribes and Pharisees Not in Kingdom:

Matt. 23:13. "But woe unto you, Scribes and Pharisees, hypocrites! for ye shut up the kingdom of heaven against men: for ye neither go in yourselves, neither suffer ye them that are entering to go in."

They Thought It Would Immediately Appear:

Lk. 19:11. "And as they heard these things, he added and spake a parable, because he was nigh to Jerusalem, and because they thought that the kingdom of God should immediately appear."

At the Institution of the Supper Christ Said:

Lk. 22:18. "For I say unto you, I will not drink of the fruit of the vine until the kingdom of God shall come."

After Christ Died.

Waited for the Kingdom:

Mk. 15:43. "Joseph of Arimathea, an honorable counselor, which also waited for the kingdom of God." Joseph was one of the disciples of Christ. Matt. 27:57.

Wilt Thou Restore the Kingdom:

Acts 1:6. "Lord, wilt thou at this time restore again the kingdom?"

If Established Before the Death, Burial, Resurrection, and Ascension of Christ, It Was:

Under the Limited Commission:

Matt. 10:5-6. "These twelve Jesus sent forth, and commanded them, saying, Go not into the way of the Gentiles, and into any city of the Samaritans enter ye not: but go rather to the lost sheep of the house of Israel."

Under the Law of Moses:

Rom. 7:4. "Wherefore, my brethren, ye also are become dead to the law by the body of Christ." Col. 2:14. "Blotting out the handwriting of ordinances that was against us, which was contrary to us, and took it out of the way, nailing it to his cross."

Before Christ Had All Power:

Matt. 28:18. "All power is given unto me in heaven and in earth."

Devil a Part Of:

Eph. 2:20. "And are built upon the foundation of the apostles and prophets, Jesus Christ himself being the chief cornerstone." If it was built during the life of Judas, since he was one of the twelve apostles, it was built upon a devil.

No Remission:

Heb. 9:22. "Without shedding of blood is no remission." Heb. 10:4. "For it is not possible that the blood of bulls and goats should take away sins." Christ shed his blood in his death. Jno. 19:34.

Without a Head:

Eph. 1:20-22. "Which he wrought in Christ, when he raised him from the dead, and set him at his own right hand in the heavenly places, far above all principality, and power, and might, and dominion, and every name that is named not only in this world, but also in that which is to come: and hath put all things under his feet, and gave him to be the head over all things to the church, which is his body." Note—(1) Raised him from the dead. (2) Set him at his right hand. (3) Put all things under his feet. (4) Gave him to be head over all things to the church.

Christ Not Priest:

Heb. 8:4. "For if he were on earth, he should not be a priest, seeing there are priests that offer gifts according to the law."

Not On Throne:

Acts 2:30-31. "Therefore being a prophet, and knowing that God had sworn with an oath to him, that of the fruit of his loins, according to the flesh, he would raise up Christ to sit on his throne; he seeing this before spake of the resurrection of Christ."

Not Redeemed:

Heb. 9:15. "And for this cause he is the mediator of the New Testament, that by means of death, for the redemption of the transgressions that were under the First Testament, they which are called might receive the promise of eternal inheritance."

Did the Twelve Apostles Constitute the Church Before the Day of Pentecost? If Yes, What About The Following:

Under the Limited Commission:

Matt. 10:5-6. "These twelve Jesus sent forth, and commanded them, saying, Go not into the way of the Gentiles, and into any city of the Samaritans enter ye not: but go rather to the lost sheep of the house of Israel."

Not Allowed to Tell That Jesus Was Christ:

Matt. 16:20. "Then charged he his disciples that they should tell no man that he was Jesus the Christ."

Peter An Offense to Christ:

Matt. 16:23. "But he turned, and said unto Peter, Get thee behind me, Satan: thou art an offense unto me: for thou savourest not the things that be of God, but those that be of men."

Not Converted:

Matt. 18:3. "Verily I say unto you, Except ye be converted, and become as little children, ye shall not enter into the kingdom of heaven."

Judas Betrays Christ:

Mk. 14:14. "And he that betrayed him had given them a token, saying, Whomsoever I shall kiss, the same is he."

59

Peter Curses and Swears and Lies:

Matt. 26:74. "Then began he to curse and to swear, saying, I know not the man."

Lost Their Hope:

Lk. 24:21. "But we trusted that it had been he which should have redeemed Israel." 1 Pet. 1:3. "Blessed be the God and Father of our Lord Jesus Christ, which according to his abundant mercy hath begotten us again unto a lively hope by the resurrection of Jesus Christ from the dead."

Do Not Believe in the Resurrection of Christ:

Lk. 24:2-11. "And they found the stone rolled away from the sepulchre. And they entered in, and found not the body of the Lord Jesus. . . . He is not here, but is risen. . . . And they returned from the sepulchre and told all these things unto the eleven, and all the rest. . . . And their words seemed to them as idle tales, and they believed them not."

Propose a Fishing Party:

Jno. 21:3. "Simon Peter saith unto them, I go a fishing. They say unto him, We also go with thee." They went forth, and entered into a ship immediately; and that night they caught nothing."

Thomas a Doubter:

Jno. 20:24-25. "But Thomas, one of the twelve called Didymus was not with them when Jesus came. The other disciples therefore said unto him, We have seen the Lord, But he said unto them, Except I shall see in his hands the prints of the nails, and put my finger into the print of the nails, and thrust my hand into his side, I will not believe."

Upbraided for Hardiness of Heart and Unbelief:

Mk. 16:14. "Afterwards he appeared unto the eleven as they sat at meat, and upbraided them with their unbelief and hardness of heart, because they believed not them which had seen him after he was risen."

After The Resurrection

The Great Commission Given:

Matt. 28:19. "Go ye therefore, and teach all nations, baptizing them in the name of the Father, and of the Son, and of the Holy Ghost."

Christ Ascends:

Acts 1:9. "And when he had spoken these things, while they beheld, he was taken up; and a cloud received him out of their sight."

Waiting for Power:

Acts 1:8. "But he shall receive power, after that the Holy Ghost is come upon you."

Matthias Selected to Fill the Place of Judas, Who Fell:

Acts 1:26. "And they gave forth their lots: and the lot fell upon Matthias; and he was numbered with the eleven apostles."

On Pentecost.

Baptized With the Holy Ghost:

Acts 2:1-4. "And when the day of Pentecost was fully come, they were all with one accord in one place. And suddenly there came a sound from heaven as of a rushing mighty wind, and it filled all the house where they were sitting. And there appeared unto them cloven tongues like as of fire, and it sat upon each of them. And they were all filled with the Holy Ghost, and began to speak with other tongues, as the Spirit gave them utterance."

Preach the Resurrection:

Acts 2:32. "This Jesus hath God raised up, whereof we all are witnesses."

The Beginning:

Acts 11:15. "And as I began to speak, the Holy Ghost fell on them, as on us at the beginning."

Added to the Church:

Acts 2:47. "And the Lord added to the church daily such as should be saved."

Who Shall Be Saved:

Mk. 16:16. "He that believeth and is baptized shall be saved."

Throne.

Oath.

Christ Promised David's Throne:

Lk. 1:32. "He shall be great, and shall be called the Son of the Highest and the Lord God shall give unto him the throne of his father David."

David's Throne Is the Lord's Throne:

1 Ki. 2:12. "Then sat Solomon upon the throne of David his father; and his kingdom was established greatly." 1 Chr. 29:23. "Then Solomon sat on the throne of the Lord as king instead of David his father."

David's Throne Is in Heaven: An Oath:

Ps. 89:35-37. "Once have I sworn by my holiness that I will not lie unto David. His seed shall endure forever, and his throne as the sun before me. It shall be established forever as the moon, and as a faithful witness in heaven." Ps. 11:4. "The Lord's throne is in heaven."

Raised—Resurrected to Sit on Throne: Another Oath:

Acts 2:30-32. "Therefore being a prophet, and knowing that God had sworn with an oath to him, that of the fruit of his loins, according to the flesh, he would raise up Christ to sit on his throne; he seeing this before spake of the resurrection of Christ, that his soul was not left in hell, neither his flesh did see corruption."

Is Seated on Throne:

Rev. 3:21. "To him that overcometh will I grant to sit with me in my throne, even as I also overcame, and am set down with my Father in his throne."

As the throne is in heaven, and Christ was to be given that throne, he could not be seated on it till he went to heaven where the throne is. But the Kingdom was to be established from the time he took the throne.

Kingdom Established: From Henceforth:"

Isa. 9:7. "Of the increase of his government and peace there shall be no end upon the throne of David, and upon his kingdom, to order it, and to establish it with judgment and with justice from henceforth even forever."

(1) God swore he would give Christ the throne of David. (2) He swore that he would resurrect Christ to sit on the throne of David. (3) The throne of David is in heaven. (4) Then Christ could not be seated on the throne till after his resurrection and ascension to heaven. (5) From "henceforth"—from the time he was seated on the throne—the kingdom was to be established. If the kingdom was established before Christ died and was resurrected, then there are two oaths that are false.

Coming of Kingdom, Power and Spirit.

Kingdom and Power to Come Together:

Mk. 9:1. "Verily I say unto you, That there be some of them that stand here, which shall not taste of death, till they have seen the kingdom of God come with power."

Power and Spirit to Come Together:

Acts 1:8. "But ye shall receive power after that the Holy Ghost is come upon you."

When Did the Spirit Come:

Acts 2:1-4. "And when the day of Pentecost was fully come, there were all with one accord in one place. And suddenly there came a sound from heaven as of a rushing mighty wind, and it filled all the house where they were sitting. And there appeared unto them cloven tongues like as of fire, and it sat upon each of them. And they were all filled with the Holy Ghost, and began to speak with other tongues, as the Spirit gave them utterance."

(1) The Kingdom and the power were to come together. (2) The power and the Spirit were to come together. (3) But the Spirit came on the first Pentecost after the resurrection of Christ: therefore, the kingdom and power came on that day.

Received Kingdom.

Given Him a Kingdom:

Dan. 7:13-14. "I saw in the night visions, and, behold, one like the Son of Man came with the clouds of heaven, and came to the Ancient of days, and they brought him near before him. And there was given him dominion, and glory, and a kingdom, that all people, nations, and languages should serve him." Note—(1) Son of man. (2) Came with the clouds of heaven. (3) Came to the Ancient of days. (4) Given him a kingdom. (5) All nations should serve him.

Went to Receive Kingdom:

Lk. 19:11-12. "And as they heard these things, he added and spake a parable, because he was nigh to Jerusalem, and because they thought that the kingdom of God should immediately appear. He said therefore, A certain nobleman went into a far country to receive for himself a kingdom, and to return."

When Did the Nobleman, Christ, Go to the Far Country:

Acts 1:9-11. "And when he had spoken these things, while they beheld, he was taken up; and a cloud received him out of their sight. And while they looked steadfastly towards heaven as he went up, behold, two men stood by them in white apparel; which also said, Ye men of Galilee, why stand ye gazing up into heaven? This same Jesus, which is taken from you into heaven, shall so come in like manner as ye have seen him go into heaven." Thus you note that after his resurrection he went into the far country, heaven; went with the clouds of heaven; came to the Ancient of days—God—and then he received the kingdom.

Kingdom—Glory.

Right Hand in Thy Kingdom:

Matt. 20:21. "Grant that these, my two sons, may sit, the one on thy right hand, and the other on thy left, in thy kingdom."

Right Hand in Thy Glory:

Mk. 10:37. "Grant unto us that we may sit, one on thy right hand, and the other on thy left hand, in thy glory."

They thought that when Christ entered into his "glory" he would then be in his kingdom, and such is the truth, or he allowed them to continue in their deception, and by his silence contributed thereto. When he entered into his glory, then he received the kingdom, but when did he enter into his glory?"

Christ Suffered—Entered Into Glory:

Lk. 24:26. "Ought not Christ to have suffered these things, and to enter into his glory?"

1 Tim. 3:16. "God was manifest in the flesh, justified in the Spirit, seen of angels, preached unto the Gentiles, believed on in the world, received up into glory."

He was not in his "glory" while on earth, nor was he in his "kingdom" while on earth.

Last Days.

Last Days—Lord's House Established:

Isa. 2:2-3. "And it shall come to pass in the last days, that the mountain of the Lord's house shall be established in the top of the mountains, and shall be exalted above the hills; and all nations shall flow unto it. And many people shall go and say, Come ye, and let us go up to the mountain of the Lord, to the house of the God of Jacob; and he will teach us of his ways, and we will walk in his paths: for out of Zion shall go forth the law, and the word of the Lord from Jerusalem."

Note—(1) Last days. (2) Lord's house shall be established. (3) All nations shall flow unto it. (4) Word of Lord go forth from Jerusalem.

On the First Pentecost After the Resurrection of Christ, Peter Said:

Acts 2:16-17. "This is that spoken by the prophet Joel; and it shall come to pass in the last days." Thus Peter calls Pentecost "last days."

What Is Lord's House:

1 Tim. 3:15. "But if I tarry long, that thou mayest know how thou oughtest to behave thyself in the house of God; which is the church of the living God." The house of God is the church of God.

Who Was Present on Pentecost When Peter Preached?

Acts 2:5-10. "And there were dwelling at Jerusalem Jews, devout men, out of every nation under heaven, . . . strangers of Rome, Jews and proselytes."

The Sermon of Peter, Preached on Pentecost, Acts 2, Was Delivered in the City of Jerusalem.

In the city of Jerusalem, on the first Pentecost after the resurrection of Christ, Peter said it was "last days;" but that is the exact time Isaiah said the house of the Lord —the church of God—would be established. But Isaiah said "all nations shall flow unto it." "All nations" could not flow during the personal ministry of Christ, for he bade his apostles: "Go not into the way of the Gentiles, and into any city of the Samaritans enter ye not; but go rather to the lost sheep of the house of Israel."

Beginning:

Acts 11:15. "And as I began to speak, the Holy Spirit fell on them as on us at the beginning." The Holy Spirit fell on them on the first Pentecost after the resurrection of Christ. Acts 2:1-4.

67

When Was the Church Built?

Will Build My Church:

Matt. 16:18. "Upon this rock I will build my church."

Can you think of a statement which will express more emphatically, in fewer words, the fact that the church was not at that time built, but was to be built at some future time? "I will build my church" cannot mean that it had been built.

It was something like eighteen months after Jesus ordained the twelve apostles (Matt. 10), and sent them forth to preach that the Lord said: "I will build my church." There are two facts revealed by the statement of the Master. (1) The church was not built at the time he made the statement, and (2) he promised to build the church.

Are Built:

Eph. 2:20. "Ye are no more strangers and foreigners but fellow citizens with the saints, and of the household of God. And are built upon the foundation of the apostles and prophets, Jesus Christ himself being the chief cornerstone."

Jesus said (Matt. 16:18), "I will build my church." Paul said (Eph. 2:20), "Ye are built." It must follow that at some time between the two statements the church was built.

Added to the Church:

Acts 2:47. "And the Lord added to the church daily such as should be saved."

In A.D. 32 Jesus said, "I will build my church." In A.D. 33 people were "added to the church." The church had been built.

The Foundation:

1 Cor. 3:11. "Other foundation can no man lay than that is laid, which is Jesus Christ."

Chief Cornerstone:

Eph. 2:20. "Jesus Christ himself being the chief cornerstone."

It Must Be a Tried Stone:

Isa. 28:16. "Behold, I lay in Zion for a foundation a stone, a tried stone, a precious cornerstone, a sure foundation."

When was the stone, Christ, "tried"? Surely the trial, the supreme test, was when he met the "strong man" in his own domain, and there conquered him. Mk. 3:27. He was declared to be all he claimed when he came forth from the grave, being "declared to be the Son of God with power, according to the spirit of holiness, by the resurrection from the dead." Rom. 1:4.

Had he failed to come forth from the dead, it would have been proof that he was an impostor, salvation would have been impossible —"if Christ be not risen, then is our preaching vain, and your faith is also vain. . . . And if Christ be not raised, your faith is vain: ye are yet in your sins." 1 Cor. 15:14-17.

If Christ had not been raised from the dead, the church of Christ could not exist today; and since the church could not exist today if Christ had not been raised, there has never been a time when the church could exist without the resurrection of Christ as an accomplished fact.

Foundation Laid at Corinth:

1 Cor. 3:11. "Other foundation can no man lay than that is laid, which is Jesus Christ."

To lay the foundation is the first work in the erection of a building.

69

What was Paul's first work when he went to Corinth?

Preached Death, Burial and Resurrection of
Christ First:

1 Cor. 15:3: "I delivered unto you first of all that which I also received, how that Christ died for our sins according to the scriptures, and that he was buried, and that he rose again the third day according to the scriptures."

In laying the foundation at Corinth the first thing Paul did was to preach the death, burial and resurrection of Christ. This being the first work in laying the foundation of the church at Corinth, it was necessarily the first work everywhere, and the church could not be builded till this foundation could be laid. But this could not be done till it was an accomplished fact. The death, burial and resurrection of Christ was first preached to the people on the first Pentecost after the resurrection of Christ. The foundation was laid, the church builded, and people added to it. Acts 2.

Head of the Corner:

Matt. 21:42. "The stone which the builders rejected, the same is become the head of the corner."

When Rejected:

Mk. 8:31. "And he began to teach them, that the Son of Man must suffer many things, and be rejected of the elders, of the chief priests, and scribes, and be killed, and after three days rise again."

Made Head After He Was Raised:

Acts 4:10-11. "Be it known unto you all, and to all the people of Israel, that by the name of Jesus Christ of Nazareth, whom ye crucified, whom God raised from the dead, even by him doth this man stand here before you whole. This is the stone which was set at nought of you builders, which is become the head of the corner."

1. Church could not be built till foundation was laid.

2. Foundation could not be laid till foundation was tried.

3. Stone could not be tried till rejected.

4. Stone was tried and proven in his resurrection.

5. It must follow that the church could not be built before Christ was raised from the dead.

COVENANTS CONTRASTED.

Old: Figure of True:

Heb. 9:24. "For Christ is not entered into the holy places made with hands, which are the figures of the true; but into heaven itself."

New: The True:

Heb. 8:1-2. "We have such an high priest, who is set on the right hand of the throne of the Majesty in the heavens; a minister of the sanctuary, and of the true tabernacle, which the Lord pitched, and not man."

Old: No Clear Conscience:

Heb. 9:8-9. "The Holy Ghost this signifying, that the way into the holiest of all was not yet made manifest, while as the first tabernacle was yet standing: which was a figure for the time then present, in which were offered both gifts and sacrifices, that could not make him that did the service perfect, as pertaining to the conscience."

New: Makes Perfect:

Heb. 7:18-19. "For there is verily a disannulling of the commandment going before for the weakness and unprofitableness thereof. For the law made nothing perfect, but the bringing in of a better hope did; by the which we draw nigh unto God."

Old: Blood of Animals:

Heb. 9:18-20. "Whereupon neither the First Testament was dedicated without blood."

"For when Moses had spoken every precept to all the people according to the law, he took the blood of calves and of goats, with water, and scarlet wool, and hyssop, and sprinkled both the book and all the people, saying, this is the blood of the testament which God hath enjoined unto you."

New: Blood of Christ:

Heb. 9:12. "Neither by the blood of goats and calves, but by his own blood he entered in once into the holy place, having obtained eternal redemption for us."

Old: Carnal Ordinances:

Heb. 9:10. "Which stood only in meats and drinks, and divers washings, and carnal ordinances, imposed on them till the time of reformation."

New: Spiritual Sacrifices:

1 Pet. 2:5. "Ye also, as lively stones are built up a spiritual house, an holy priesthood, to offer up spiritual sacrifices."

Old: Purifying Flesh:

Heb. 9:13. "For if the blood of bulls and of goats, and the ashes of an heifer sprinkling the unclean, sanctifieth to the purifying of the flesh."

New: Purifying Soul:

1 Pet. 1:22. "Seeing ye have purified your souls in obeying the truth."

Old: Priests Died:

Heb. 7:23. "And they truly were many priests, because they were not suffered to continue by reason of death."

New: Our Priest Continueth Ever:

Heb. 7:24. "But this man, because he continueth ever, hath an unchangeable priesthood."

Old: Faulty:

Heb. 8:7. "For if the first covenant had been faultless, then should no place have been sought for the second."

New: Better:

Heb. 8:6. "But now hath he obtained a more excellent ministry, by how much also he is the mediator of a better covenant, which was established upon better promises." The New is Perfect, Jas. 1:25. "But whoso looketh into the perfect law of liberty."

Old: Taken Away:

Heb. 10:9. "Then said he, Lo, I come to do thy will, O God. He taketh away the first, that he may establish the second."

New: Establish:

Heb. 10:9. "He taketh away the first, that he may establish the second."

Old: Temporal Inheritance:

Ps. 105:9-11. "Unto thee will I give the land of Canaan, the lot of your inheritance."

New: Eternal Inheritance:

1 Pet. 1:4. "To an inheritance incorruptible, and undefiled, and that fadeth not away, reserved in heaven for you."

New Or Old.

New Man:

Eph. 2:15. "Having abolished in his flesh the enmity, even the law of commandments contained in ordinances; for to make in himself of twain one new man, so making peace."

New Name:

Acts 11:26: "And the disciples were called Christians first in Antioch."

New Religion:

Gal. 1:13-23. "For ye have heard of my conversation in time past in the Jews' religion, how that beyond measure I persecuted the church of God, and wasted it. . . . But they heard only, That he which persecuted us in times past now preacheth the faith which once he destroyed."

New Covenant:

Heb. 8:6-8. "But now hath he obtained a more excellent ministry, by how much also he is the mediator of a better covenant, which was established upon better promises. For if the first covenant had been faultless, then should no place have been sought for the second. For finding fault with them, he saith, Behold, the days come, saith the Lord, when I will make a new covenant with the house of Israel and with the house of Judah."

New Laws:

Rom. 8:2. "For the law of the Spirit of life in Christ Jesus hath made me free from the law of sin and death."

New Mediator:

Heb. 12:24. "And to Jesus the mediator of the new covenant."

New and Living Way:

Heb. 10:19-20. "Having therefore, brethren, boldness to enter into the holiest by the blood of Jesus, by a new and living way, which he hath consecrated for us, through the veil, that is to say, his flesh."

New King:

Rev. 1:5. "And from Jesus Christ, who is the faithful witness, and the first begotten of the dead, and the prince of the kings of the earth."

New Priest:

Heb. 7:28. "For the law maketh men high priests which have infirmity; but the word of the oath, which was since the law, maketh the Son, who is consecrated for evermore."

New Sacrifice:

1 Pet. 2:5. "Ye also, as lively stones, are built up a spiritual house, an holy priesthood, to offer up spiritual sacrifices, acceptable to God by Jesus Christ."

CONFESSION

Christ Promises to Confess You:

Matt. 10:32-33. Whosoever therefore shall confess me before men, him will I confess before my Father which is in heaven."

Confess You Before the Angels:

Lk. 12:8. "Whosoever shall confess me before men, him shall the Son of man also confess before the angels of God."

Confess Unto Salvation:

Rom. 10:9-10. "If thou shalt confess with thy mouth the Lord Jesus, and shalt believe in thine heart that God hath raised him from the dead, thou shalt be saved. For with the heart man believeth unto righteousness; and with the mouth confession is made unto salvation."

Note: Christ commanded the disciples to teach all nations, and to baptize the believers. Before one can be baptized he must be a believer, and in making the confession that fact is made known, and is "unto salvation." When the nobleman from Ethiopia wished to be baptized, the preacher, Philip, consented to baptize him if he was a believer. Acts 8:36.

ARE WE HEREDITARILY TOTALLY DEPRAVED?

"*Hereditarily:* By inheritance; by right of descent."—Webster.

"*Totally:* Wholly; entirely; fully; completely."—Webster.

"*Depraved:* Made bad or worse; vitiated; tainted; corrupted. 2. Corrupt; wicked; destitute of holiness or good principles."—Webster.

We Are Offspring of God:

Acts 17:29. "Forasmuch then as we are the offspring of God." Certainly it is not the body—the flesh—that is the "offspring of God." Are you ready to insist that the spirit comes from God depraved?

God Father of Spirits:

Heb. 12:9. "Furthermore we have had fathers of the flesh which corrected us, and we gave them reverence: shall we not much rather be in subjection unto the Father of spirits and live?" Here the father of the flesh is contrasted with the Father of the spirit.

76

God is the Father of the spirit. Is God the Father of a totally depraved spirit?

God Gives the Spirit:

Eccl. 12:7. "Then shall the dust return to the earth as it was: and the Spirit shall return to God who gave it." Does God give a totally depraved spirit?

Become as Little Children:

Matt. 18:3. "Verily I say unto you, Except ye be converted, and become as little children, ye shall not enter into the kingdom of heaven." If the child is born totally depraved, then we must become like it—totally depraved—or it will not be possible to enter the kingdom.

Gone Out of the Way:

Rom. 3:12. "They are all gone out of the way, they are together become unprofitable." "Become unprofitable"—not born that way.

Don't Bear Iniquity of Father:

Ezk. 18:20. "The son shall not bear the iniquity of the father, neither shall the father bear the iniquity of the son."

I think the above scriptures will convince you that man is not wholly bad by inheritance or descent. Sin is a principle that exists only as the result of unlawful, unrighteous acts performed by one who has the power to discern between right and wrong. "Sin: n. The voluntary departure of a moral agent from a known rule of rectitude or duty, prescribed by God; any voluntary transgression of the divine law or violation of a divine command. v. i. To depart voluntarily from the path of duty prescribed by God to man; to violate the divine law in any particular." —Webster. Not one single item of this definition can be received or transmitted by inheritance. Each item shows individual responsibility. Before one can be a sinner, either in the sight of God or man, they must have the power of reason. Deprive one of the power of reason and they cannot have the slightest conception of right or wrong. They are not held amenable to the law of God or man. They are not and cannot be subjects of the law. As sin is the "voluntary departure" from the law, since infants and idiots have no power to reason or will, or desire to depart from the law, it follows that they cannot be sinners. To say that I am a sinner by inheritance, or that I was born a sinner, since sin is the transgression of the law (1 Jno. 3:4), is to declare that I transgressed the law of God before I was born.

Many do not know what is meant by "Inheritant Depravity," and for that reason I give a quotation from Mr. John Wesley's Sermons, Vol. 2, page 266: "In Adam all died, all human kind, all the children of men who were in Adam's loins. The natural consequences of this is, that every one descended from him comes into the world spiritually dead, dead to God, wholly dead in sin; entirely void of the image of God, of all the righteousness and holiness wherein Adam was created. Instead of this, every man born into the world now bears the image of the devil, in pride and self-will; the image of the beast, in sensual appetites and desires." In his work on Original Sins, page 340, he says: "We are condemned before we have done good or evil; under the curse ere we know what it is."

Dr. W. A. Jarrell, Missionary Baptist, in "Gospel in Water," says: "That man is totally depraved is evident from his being a child of the devil—fathered by the devil of the same moral nature." (Pages 251, 252).

Reader, do you think this a dark picture? Well, it is just what is meant by being "Hereditarily Totally Depraved."

As sin is "voluntarily" transgression of the law, if the child is born "wholly corrupt," since one cannot be "wholly corrupt" till they have violated every law of right, then this ungodly theory teaches that an unborn infant has violated every known law of right. Don't shudder at this. It proves more. A child cannot inherit from its parents property they do not possess. The child, at least, inherits its physical organism from its earthly parents. The Holy Spirit says: "The works of the flesh are manifest, which are these: Adultery, fornication, uncleanness, lasciviousness, idolatry, witchcraft, hatred, variance, emulations, wrath, strife, seditions, heresies, envyings, murders, drunkenness, revelings, and such like: . . . they which do such things shall not enter the kingdom of God." Gal. 5:19-21. The above sins are works of the flesh, and the parent gives the child its physical organism. If the child is born "totally depraved," since the parent cannot give to the child that which they do not possess, then the parents must possess the above sins; yes, with an extra supply, for some of them have a dozen children.

Let us look at one or two of the passages that are relied on to prove that children are born "totally depraved." "Behold I was shapen in iniquity; and in sin did my mother conceive me." Psa. 51:5. Note—David had no existence before conception. The "iniquity" existed when he was shapen, and the sin existed when he was "conceived." As he had

79

no existence before "conception," and as he existed at the time of "conception," you cannot fail to see that the sin existed before David had an existence even by conception. There is no intimation in this passage that David was born a sinner, or with a sinful nature.

"The wicked are estranged from the womb; they go astray as soon as they be born, speaking lies." Ps. 58:3. This declares that they were not "born astray." They went astray, after birth. This "going astray" was "speaking lies," or lying. As lying is sin and sin is "voluntarily" departure from the law of God, then when they went astray they were old enough to "voluntarily" depart from the law of God. "Voluntary. Willing; proceeding from free-will." Of their own "free-will" they spoke lies, thus became sinners.

IS ETERNAL LIFE CONDITIONAL?

Believeth—May Have Life:
Jno. 6:40. "And this is the will of him that sent me, that every one which seeth the Son, and believeth on him, may have everlasting life."

Believing—Might Have Life:
Jno. 20:31. "But these are written, that ye might believe that Jesus is the Christ, the Son of God; and that believing ye might have life through his name."

Repentance Unto Life:
Acts 11:18. "Then hath God also to the Gentiles granted repentance unto life."

Come—Have Life:
Jno. 5:40. "And ye will not come to me, that ye might have life."

Render Life:

Rom. 2:6-7. "Who will render to every man according to his deeds: to them who by patient continuance in well doing seek for glory and honor and immortality, eternal life."

From the above scripture you cannot fail to learn that eternal life is conditional. A few thoughts in connection with the same may be well.

"Then Paul and Barnabas waxed bold, and said, It was necessary that the word of God should first have been spoken to you; but seeing ye put it from you, and judge yourself unworthy of everlasting life, lo, we turn to the Gentiles." Acts 13:46. Again: "Be it known therefore unto you that the salvation of God is sent unto the Gentiles, and that they will hear it." Acts 28:28.

Note: The word of God was to be preached to the Jews first, they "put it from" them —rejected it, and in so doing, counted "themselves unworthy of everlasting life." Here eternal life is clearly conditioned on receiving the word of God. When the Jews refused to accept the word, and by so doing receive eternal life, Paul said, "Lo, we turn to the Gentiles." Why turn to the Gentiles? "Be it known therefore unto you, that the salvation of God is sent unto the Gentiles, and that they will hear it." Acts 28:28. What did they hear? "The word of God should have first been spoken to you [Jews]" (Acts 13:46), but as you will not receive it, we will take salvation to the Gentiles, and they will hear it. Again, speaking of the Jews, Paul says: "Forbidding us to speak to the Gentiles that they might be saved." 1 Thess. 2:16. Salvation was sent to the Gentiles. When the

81

Jews refused the word of God, Paul says: "Lo, we turn to the Gentiles." God sent salvation—the means of salvation—to them by Paul. Paul declares the Jews forbade him to speak to the Gentiles that they might be saved. 1. The Gentiles were not saved. 2. Paul carries salvation (the means of salvation) to them. 3. That they might be saved it was necessary that Paul should speak the word of the Lord to them. 4. They must hear—accept —it, or be like the Jews, put it from them, and thus be accounted unworthy of "eternal life." This is quite sufficient to convince you that eternal life is conditional; but another quotation, that you may be assured that life and death, good and evil, are matters of choice on the part of man. "I will call heaven and earth to record this day against you, that I have set before you life and death, blessings and cursing: therefore choose life, that both thou and thy seed may live." Deut. 30:19.

"See, I have set before thee this day life and good, and death and evil; in that I command thee this day to love the Lord thy God, to walk in his ways, and to keep his commandments and his statutes and judgments, that thou mayest live and multiply" (vs. 15-16). That life is here made conditional needs not a comment.

When Do We Receive Eternal Life?

Hope of Eternal Life:

Tit. 1:2. "In hope of eternal life, which God, that cannot lie, promised before the world began."

Hope of Eternal Life:

Tit. 3:7. "That being justified by his grace, we should be made heirs according to the hope of eternal life."

Promised to Christians:

1 Jno. 2:25. "And this is the promise that he hath promised us, even eternal life."

After the Fight of Faith:

1 Tim. 6:12. "Fight the good fight of faith, lay hold on eternal life, whereunto thou art called."

In the Time to Come:

1 Tim. 6:19. "Laying up in store for themselves a good foundation against the time to come, that they may lay hold on eternal life."

Sow to the Spirit, Then We Reap:

Gal. 6:8. "For he that soweth to the flesh shall of the flesh reap corruption; but he that soweth to the spirit shall of the spirit reap life everlasting."

In the World to Come:

Mk. 10:29-30. "And Jesus answered and said, Verily I say unto you, There is no man that hath left house, or brethren, or sisters, or father, or mother, or wife, or children, or lands, for my sake, and the gospel's, but he shall receive an hundred fold now in this time, houses and brethren, and lands, with persecutions; and in the world to come eternal life."

Life to Come:

1 Tim. 4:8. "Having promise of the life that now is, and of that which is to come."

After the Resurrection;

Jno. 5:28-29. "For the hour is coming, in which all that are in the graves shall hear his voice, and shall come forth; they that have done good, unto the resurrection of life."

After the Judgment:

Matt. 25:46. "And these shall go away into everlasting punishment: but the righteous into life eternal."

End:

Rom. 6:22. "But now being made free from sin, and become the servants of God, ye have your fruit unto holiness, and the end everlasting life."

Not only does Christ declare that eternal life is to be received in the world to come, Paul clearly teaches the same.

From nature each day you learn the lesson that you first sow, then comes the time of reaping. The most ignorant know this. Listen: "He that soweth to the flesh shall of the flesh reap corruption; but he that soweth to the Spirit shall of the Spirit reap life everlasting." Gal. 6:8. That the sinner is "sowing to the flesh" is admitted by all. When they become Christians, they begin to "sow to the Spirit," and the reaping time will come—they will receive eternal life in the world to come. If man receives eternal life the moment he believes, someone should tell when he sowed to the Spirit, that he might reap the everlasting life. Additional comment is unnecessary.

FAITH.

Defined:

Heb. 11:1. "Now faith is the substance of things hoped for, the evidence of things not seen."

It Is a Work:

Jno. 6:29. "Jesus answered and said unto them, This is the work of God, that ye believe on him whom he hath sent."

It Is A Full Persuasion:

Rom. 4:20-21. "He staggered not at the promise of God through unbelief; but was strong in faith, giving glory to God; and being fully persuaded that, what he promised, he was able to perform."

How Do We Get Faith?

Written That Ye Might Believe:

Jno. 20:30-31. "And many other signs truly did Jesus in the presence of his disciples, which are not written in this book: but these are written, that ye might believe that Jesus is the Christ, the Son of God."

Heard Him—Believe:

Jno. 4:42. "Now we believe, not because of thy sayings: for we have heard him ourselves."

Hear—Believe:

Acts 15:7. "God made choice among us, that the Gentiles by my mouth should hear the word of the gospel and believe."

So Spake—They Believed:

Acts 14:1. "And it came to pass in Iconium, that they went both together into the synagogue of the Jews, and so spake, that a great multitude both of the Jews and also of the Greeks believed."

Hearing—Believed:

Acts 18:8. "And many of the Corinthians hearing believed, and were baptized."

Faith Comes by Hearing:

Rom. 10:14-17. "And how shall they believe in him of whom they have not heard? . . . So then faith cometh by hearing, and hearing by the word of God."

Faith cannot be produced in the absence of testimony.

All are agreed that one must have faith, or be lost.

Man is saved by faith, but Christ is the Savior. It follows, then, since Christ is the Savior and we are saved by faith, that Christ is the author of our faith.

Faith comes by hearing the word of God. Rom. 10:17. Jesus is the author and finisher of (the) our faith. Heb. 12:2. As I am saved by faith, and faith comes by hearing the word of God, and Jesus is the author and finisher of our faith; surely he is the author of the words which produce faith. God said to Moses, "I will raise them up a Prophet from among their brethren, like unto thee, and will put my words in his mouth; and he shall speak unto them all that I shall command him. And it shall come to pass, that whosoever will not hearken unto my words which he shall speak in my name, I will require it of him." Deut. 18:18-19. Peter, referring to this prophecy, says it had reference to Christ. "For Moses truly said unto the fathers, A prophet shall the Lord thy God raise up unto you of your brethren, like unto me; him shall ye year in all things whatsoever he shall say unto you. And it shall come to pass that every soul which will not hear that prophet shall be destroyed from among the people." Acts 3:22-23.

God was to raise up Christ and give him his word. Faith comes by hearing the word of God. Did the Father give Jesus the word? "For I have given unto them [apostles] the words which thou gavest me." Jno. 17:8. Christ gave the apostles the words God gave him. "Neither pray I for these alone, but for them also which shall believe on me through their words." Jno. 17:20. God gave the words to Christ, he gave them to the apostles. Our faith comes by hearing their words, and Christ prays for those who believe on him through the words they speak.

Though we have learned who we must hear, that we may believe, when must we hear them? Certainly when they become witnesses of Christ. If you do not believe the testimony God has given of his Son, you are condemned. I must receive the word. "When ye receive the word of God, which ye heard of us, ye received it not as the word of men, but as it is in truth, the word of God, which [word] effectually worketh also in you that believe." 1 Thess. 2:13. Jesus said to the apostles: "Ye shall be witnesses" after that the Holy Spirit is come upon you." Acts 1:8. Since I am to believe on Christ through the testimony of the apostles, and they were not to be witnesses till the Holy Spirit came upon them, it is certain that I must hear what they say after they became witnesses—my faith must come by hearing the word of God, the word that God gave Christ, and Christ gave the apostles. My faith must come in this way only.

But the apostles who had the word of Jesus said for us to repent. Then I must believe and repent, or perish. They said I must confess my faith in him. The apostles who had the words of Jesus said I must be baptized for the "remission of sins."

God has never blessed any man on the condition of the man's faith before his faith expressed itself in some act.

87

Faith and Belief.

"Faith" is a noun. "Believe" is a verb. So far as the mental act is counted, they are the same. The words are used interchangeably.

Matt. 8:10-13. "Verily I say unto you, I have not found so great faith, no, not in Israel. . . . And Jesus said unto the centurion, Go thy way; and as thou hast believed, so be it done unto thee."

Jno. 20:27. "Then said he to Thomas, Reach hither thy finger, and behold my hands; and reach hither thy hand, and thrust it into my side: and be not faithless, but believing."

Is Faith Necessary To Salvation?

Believe—Shall Be Saved:
Acts 16:30-31. "Sirs, what must I do to be saved? And they said, Believe on the Lord Jesus Christ, and thou shalt be saved, and thy house."

Gospel Saves Believers:
Rom. 1:16. "I am not ashamed of the gospel of Christ: for it is the power of God unto salvation to every one that believeth."

Save Them That Believe:
1 Cor. 1:21. "It pleased God by the foolishness of preaching to save them that believe."

Believeth—Receive Remission of Sins:
Acts 10:43. "To him give all the prophets witness, that through his name whosoever believeth in him shall receive remission of sins."

Justified by Faith:
Rom. 5:1. "Therefore being justified by faith, we have peace with God."

Will Faith Only Save?

Faith Without Love Will Not Profit:

1 Cor. 13:2. "Though I have all faith, so that I could remove mountains, and have not charity, I am nothing."

The Cowardly Rulers Believed:

Jno. 12:42-44. "Nevertheless among the chief rulers also many believed on him; but because of the Pharisees they did not confess him, lest they should be put out of the synagogue: for they loved the praise of men more than the praise of God."

Faith Alone Is Dead:

Jas. 2:17. "Even so faith, if it hath not works, is dead, being alone."

The Devils Believed:

Jas. 2:19. "Thou believest there is one God; thou doest well: the devils also believe, and tremble."

Faith Without Works Is Dead:

Jas. 2:20. "But wilt thou know, O vain man, that faith without works is dead?"

Not Justified By Faith Only:

Jas. 2:24. "Ye see then how that by works a man is justified, and not by faith only."

Faith Without Works Is Dead:

Jas. 2:26. "For as the body without the spirit is dead, so faith without works is dead also."

The Faith That Avails Must Work:

Gal. 5:6. "For in Jesus Christ neither circumcision availeth anything, nor uncircumcision, but faith which worketh by love." Since the faith must "work" by love, before it will "avail," then "faith" cannot save the moment one has "faith," for there must be some time in which "faith" "works" before it saves—avails.

Saved Or Justified By.

God:

"Rom. 8:33. "It is God that justifieth."

Christ:

Matt. 1:21. "And thou shalt call his name Jesus: for he shall save his people from their sins."

Spirit:

1 Cor. 6:11. "But ye are justified in the name of the Lord Jesus, and by the Spirit of our God."

Blood:

Rom. 5:9. "Much more then, being now justified by his blood, we shall be saved from wrath through him."

Grace:

Rom. 3:24. "Being justified freely by his grace through the redemption that is in Christ Jesus."

Gospel:

1 Cor. 15:1-2. "I declare unto you the gospel which I preached unto you, which also ye have received, and wherein ye stand; by which also ye are saved."

Mercy:

Tit. 3:4-5. "But after that the kindness and love of God our Savior towards man appeared, not by works of righteousness which we have done but according to his mercy he saved us."

Faith:

Rom. 5:1. "Therefore being justified by faith, we have peace with God."

Hope:

Rom. 8:24. "For we are saved by hope."

Works:

Jas. 2:24. "Ye see then how that by works a man is justified, and not by faith only."

Baptism:

1 Pet. 3:19-21. "By which also he went and preached unto the spirits in prison; which sometimes were disobedient, when once the long suffering of God waited in the days of Noah, while the ark was a preparing, wherein few, that is, eight souls were saved by water. The like figure whereunto even baptism doth also now save us (not the putting away of the filth of the flesh, but the answer of a good conscience towards God), by the resurrection of Jesus Christ."

Most certainly we are not "justified by faith only."

Though the Bible teaches that we are "justified by faith"—saved by faith—faith is not the Savior. Christ is the Savior. Faith is means to reach the end—salvation in Christ. Man is saved by repentance, but repentance is not the Savior; it, too, is a means to the end—salvation in Christ. Man is saved by the confession, also by baptism, yet these cannot be Saviors. The Savior is a person, a being. Faith, repentance, confession and baptism are acts performed which are necessary to reach salvation in Christ the Savior.

Many are confused by not understanding at what point man is justified by faith. Some think it is the moment you believe in Christ. Others insist that it is not till your faith has expressed itself in obedience to Christ.

The apostle says: "Abraham believed God, and it [faith] was counted unto him for righteousness." Rom. 4:3. How long was his faith "counted" for righteousness? "Was not

Abraham our father justified by works when he had offered Isaac his son upon the altar? Seest thou how faith wrought with his works, and by works was faith made perfect? And the scripture was fulfilled which saith, Abraham believed God, and it was imputed unto him for righteousness." Jas. 2:21-23. You cannot fail to learn the lesson that God does not accept a man till his faith is made perfect by works, or through obedience.

Man is saved by faith. "And being made perfect, he became the author of eternal salvation unto all them that obey him." Heb. 5:9. Though man is saved by faith, you will not fail to see that his faith must lead him through obedience before he is saved.

What of Disbelievers—Those Without Faith?

Without Faith—Can't Please God:

Heb. 11:6. "But without faith it is impossible to please him: for he that cometh to God must believe that he is, and that he is a rewarder of them that diligently seek him."

Believe Not—Shall Be Damned:

Mk. 16:16. "He that believeth not shall be damned."

Believe Not—Condemned:

Jno. 3:18. "He that believeth not is condemned already, because he hath not believed in the name of the only begotten Son of God."

Disbelievers—Not See Life:

Jno. 3:36. "He that believeth not the Son shall not see life; but the wrath of God abideth on him."

Believe Not—Die in Sins:

Jno. 8:24. "For if ye believe not that I am he, ye shall die in your sins."

THE GOSPEL

Power of God to Save:

Rom. 1:16. "For I am not ashamed of the gospel of Christ: for it is the power of God unto salvation to every one that believeth."

Gospel of Salvation:

Eph. 1:13. "In whom ye also trusted after that ye heard the word of truth, the gospel of your salvation."

Called by the Gospel:

2 Thess. 2:13-14. "God hath from the beginning chosen you to salvation through sanctification of the Spirit and belief of the truth: whereunto he called you by our gospel."

Begotten Through the Gospel:

1 Cor. 4:15. "For though ye have ten thousand instructors in Christ, yet have ye not many fathers: for in Christ Jesus I have begotten you through the gospel."

Faith Comes by the Gospel:

Acts 15:7. "Ye know how that a good while ago God made choice among us, that the Gentiles by my mouth should hear the word of the gospel, and believe."

Partake of Promises by the Gospel:

Eph. 3:6. "The Gentiles should be fellow heirs and of the same body, and partakers of his promise in Christ by the gospel."

Must Obey the Gospel:

Rom. 10:16. "But they have not all obeyed the gospel."

Punishment for Not Obeying the Gospel:

2 Thess. 1:8. "Taking vengeance on them that know not God, and that obey not the gospel of our Lord Jesus Christ."

Obey Not Gospel—What the End:

1 Pet. 4:17. "Judgment must begin at the house of God: and if it first begin at us, what shall the end be of them that obey not the gospel of God."

Another Gospel:

Gal. 1:6-9. "I marvel that ye are so soon removed from him that called you into the grace of Christ unto another gospel: which is not another; but there be some that trouble you, and would pervert the gospel of Christ. But though we or an angel from heaven preach any other gospel unto you than that which we have preached unto you, let him be accursed. As we said before, so say I now again, If any man preach any other gospel unto you than that ye have received, let him be accursed."

I am ready to preach the Gospel
to you that are at Rome also.
For I am not Ashamed
of the gospel of Christ: for
it is the powEr of God unto salvation.
Rom. 1:15-16

You understand that "gospel" means "good news"—good news about Christ and how to be saved in him. Preaching the gospel is teaching the gospel. "It pleased God by the foolishness of preaching [the gospel] to save them that believe." 1 Cor. 1:21. To teach the gospel is to cause people to understand. The apostle says you must see, hear and understand. Then we are to teach the gospel that it may be understood. Having heard and

94

understood the gospel, you believe it. But being taught law, hearing, understanding and believing is not obeying the law. Man may be taught law, understand and believe in every principle set forth, and justice of said law, yet violate every precept of law and justice. So it is with the gospel. We may teach it, people may believe and understand it, and refuse through life to obey it. Hence, to believe the gospel is not to obey it. Believing only places one in position where they can obey the gospel. There is no degree of faith that will bring man to salvation, except that faith which is perfected by obeying the gospel. God takes vengeance on "all who obey not the gospel" (2 Thess. 2:8); but God takes vengeance on none but sinners. Then it must follow, that though a man hears, understands and believes the gospel, he is a sinner till he obeys.

Paul says: "For I am not ashamed of the gospel of Christ: for it is the power of God unto salvation." Rom. 1:16. As there is no power to save greater than God's power, and the gospel is the power of God, then there is no power greater than God's power—the gospel—to bring man to salvation. If it takes more than the gospel to bring man to salvation, then God's power is not sufficient, seeing the gospel is God's power. What do you think of a man who will pray to God to send down a power from heaven to aid his power—the gospel—in converting and saving souls?

Man must believe on the Christ of the gospel before he can obey his commands as taught in the gospel. Christ sent his apostles to preach (teach) us what we ought to do. They told of Christ, and how to obtain salvation through obedience to him. The one who believes can, by faith, see freedom from sin. With joy he accepts, obeys, and rejoices in freedom from sin.

Ask a child of God: How were you saved? He will reply: By the power of God. He understands that when he obeyed the gospel he utilized the power of God to reach the goal —salvation. He knows he cannot obey his own faith; but he knows that he can obey God by faith. The obedience to the gospel is the result of faith, and is called faithfulness. As my act of believing the gospel is simply the mind seeing, understanding, accepting the gospel as the means ordained of God by which I reach salvation; then I walk by faith in obeying the gospel; by faith, now, I see, I have only by the power of God, reached the goal—salvation.

My act of believing what God says to me cannot be the thing said. My act of believing the gospel cannot be the gospel. For this reason my act of believing cannot be the power of God, for the gospel is the power of God. Then it must follow that I am not saved simply by my act of believing, but am saved by the power of God—the gospel—when I by faith utilize the power. In obeying the gospel, then, I am saved by the power of God. Reader, from a heart of faith and love obey the gospel, and thus avail yourself of the power of God, and be saved.

The Gospel, Law of the Lord, Word of God.

God's Saving Power is in the Gospel:

Mk. 16:15-16. "Preach the gospel to every creature. He that believeth and is baptized shall be saved; but he that believeth not shall be damned."

Rom. 1:16. "For I am not ashamed of the gospel of Christ: for it is the power of God unto salvation to every one that believeth."

God's Converting Power:

Ps. 19:7. "The law of the Lord is perfect, converting the soul."

Frees From Sin:

Rom. 8:2. "For the law of the Spirit of life in Christ Jesus hath made me free from the law of sin and death."

Word is a Fire and Hammer:

Jer. 23:29. "Is not my word like a fire? saith the Lord; and like a hammer that breaketh the rock in pieces?"

Word of Reconciliation:

2 Cor. 5:18. "And hath committed unto us the word of reconciliation."

Faith Producing Power:

Rom. 10:17. "Faith cometh by hearing, and hearing by the word of God."

The Word Sanctifies:

Jno. 17:17. "Sanctify them through thy truth: thy word is truth."

Word of God is Seed:

Lk. 8:11. "The seed is the word of God." The seed produced some an hundredfold, some sixtyfold, some thirtyfold.

The Word of God Works:

1 Thess. 2:13. "The word of God, which effectually worketh also in you that believe."

The Word Builds:

Acts 20:32. "I commend you to God, and to the word of his grace, which is able to build you up, and to give you an inheritance among all them that are sanctified."

Obey the Gospel, or Be Destroyed:

2 Thess. 1:8. "Taking vengeance on them that know not God, and that obey not the gospel of our Lord Jesus Christ."

Judged by the Word:

Jno. 12:48. "The word that I have spoken, the same shall judge him in the last day."

Do Commandments to Enter City:

Rev. 22:14. "Blessed are they who do his commandments, that they may have right to the tree of life, and may enter in through the gates into the city. For without are dogs and sorcerers."

The death, burial, and resurrection of Christ are the fundamental facts of the gospel (1 Cor. 15:1-4), and Christ commanded that the gospel be preached to every creature, and promised to save those who believe and obey it—those who live according to its teaching.

The gospel is the product of the Godhead, and was given to man after four thousand years of man's history. It is the perfect system for the redemption of man, and contains the power of God for man's salvation. Rom. 1:16.

He who attempts to change the facts, commands, or promises of the gospel is condemned. Gal. 1:7-8. "There be some that trouble you, and would pervert the gospel of Christ. But though we or an angel from heaven, preach any other gospel unto you than that we have preached unto you, let him be accursed."

Preach the Gospel:

Mk. 16:15-16. "Preach the gospel to every creature. He that believeth and is baptized shall be saved."

98

Paul says the Jews forbade him "to speak to the Gentiles that they might be saved." 1 Thess. 2:16. Preach the gospel.

You can believe facts, but you do not obey facts.

We are saved when we "obey the truths" (1 Pet. 1:22), not when we believe the facts.

GRACE.

For the **G**race of
GOd that bringeth
Salvation hath
a**P**peared to all men,
teaching us that d**E**nying ungodliness and worldly
lusts, we should **L**ive soberly. —Tit. 2:11-12.

Grace Came by Christ:
Jno. 1:17. "The law was given by Moses, but grace and truth came by Jesus Christ."

Grace Teaches:
Tit. 2:11. "For the grace of God that bringeth salvation hath appeared to all men, teaching us."

Saved by Grace:
Eph. 2:5. "By grace ye are saved."

Stand in Grace:
Rom. 5:2. "By whom also we have access by faith into this grace wherein we stand."

Fallen From Grace:
Gal. 5:4. "Christ has become of no effect unto you, whosoever of you are justified by the law; ye are fallen from grace."

Are We Saved by Grace Alone?

If we are saved by grace alone, then all men will be saved, and the doctrine of the Universalists is right, for:

Tit. 2:11. "For the grace of God that bringeth salvation hath appeared to all men."

Grace and the Gospel

We Stand in Grace:

Rom. 5:2. "By whom also we have access by faith into this grace wherein we stand."

We Stand in the Gospel:

1 Cor. 15:1. "Moreover, brethren, I declare unto you the gospel which I preached unto you, which also ye have received, and wherein ye stand."

We Are Saved by Grace:

Eph. 2:5. "By grace ye are saved."

We Are Saved by the Gospel:

1 Cor. 15:2. "Moreover, brethren I declare unto you the gospel which I preached unto you, which also ye have received, and wherein ye stand; by which also ye are saved."

THE GREAT COMMISSION.

The Limited Commission:

Matt. 10:5-6. "These twelve Jesus sent forth, and commanded them, saying, Go not into the way of the Gentiles, and into any of the cities of the Samaritans enter ye not; but go rather to the lost sheep of the house of Israel."

In the foregoing Jesus circumscribed the preaching of the apostles. They were not allowed to preach to the Gentiles, nor to the Samaritans. They were commanded to preach to the "lost sheep of the house of Israel" only. For this reason this is called the "Limited Commission."

After his resurrection Jesus gave what is called the Great Commission, the World-Wide Commission, the Last Commission.

The Great Commission:

Matt. 28:18-19. "Go ye therefore, and teach all nations, baptizing them in the name of the Father, and of the Son, and of the Holy Ghost: teaching them to observe all things whatsoever I have commanded you: and lo, I am with you always, even unto the end of the world."

Mk. 16:15-16. "Go into all the world, and preach the gospel to every creature. He that believeth and is baptized shall be saved; but he that believeth not shall be damned."

Lk. 24:46-49. "And he said unto them, Thus it is written, and thus it behooved Christ to suffer, and to rise from the dead the third day: and that repentance and remission of sins should be preached in his name among all nations, beginning at Jerusalem. And ye are witnesses of these things. And, behold, I send the promise of my Father upon you: but tarry ye in the city of Jerusalem, until ye be endued with power from on high."

From these three records of the Commission it is learned that the following items are mentioned:

(1) Preaching, (2) Believing, (3) Repentance, (4) Baptism, (5) Salvation, or remission of sins.

There has been much disputing as to the order in which these items should come: *i.e.*, do people "believe" before they "repent," or does "repentance" come before "faith"? Does salvation come before baptism, or must one be baptized to be saved?

101

With all the disputing about the order in which the acts must come, there is agreement that the Commission mentioned Preaching, Repentance, Baptism, Salvation, or remission of sins.

The Commission Executed:

The apostles began work under this commission on the first Pentecost after the resurrection of Christ. They were guided by the Holy Spirit in their work. The history of their preaching and the obedience rendered to their preaching is recorded in the book of Acts. The record as found in this book will certainly give us the divine interpretation of the Great Commission. Notice the conversions mentioned in the following passages, just what occurred, and you will find it is in perfect harmony with the Commission. Too, it will be learned in what order the items mentioned came.

Acts 2:14-38. (1) Preaching, (2) Repentance, (3) Baptism, (4) Remission of Sins.

Acts 8:5-12. (1) Preaching, (2) Believing, (3) Baptism.

Acts 8:26-38. (1) Preaching, (2) Believing, (3) Baptism.

Acts 10 and 11. (1) Preaching, (2) Repentance, (3) Baptism.

Acts 16:14-15. (1) Preaching, (2) Baptism.

Acts 16:25-33. (1) Preaching, (2) Believing, (3) Baptism.

Acts 18:8. (1) Hearing, (2) Believed, (3) Baptism.

Acts 19:1-5. (1) Preaching, (2) Believing, (3) Baptism.

Acts 22:12-16. (1) Preaching, (2) Baptism, (3) Wash Away Sins.

(For a discussion of the Great Commission, see the author's *Sound Doctrine*, Vol. 1.)

————

THE HEART—WHAT IT DOES.

Thinks:

Matt. 9:4. "And Jesus knowing their thoughts said, Wherefore think ye evil in your hearts."

Understands:

Isa. 32:4. "The heart also of the rash shall understand knowledge."

Knows:

Prov. 14:10. "The heart knoweth his own bitterness."

Believes:

Rom. 10:10. "For with the heart man believeth unto righteousness."

Doubts:

Mk. 11:23. "And shall doubt in his heart."

Purposes:

2 Cor. 9:7. "Every man according as he purposeth in his heart, so let him give."

Deviseth:

Prov. 16:9. "A man's heart deviseth his way."

Reasons:

Mk. 2:6. "But there were certain of the scribes sitting there, and reasoning in their hearts."

Desires:

Rom. 10:1. "Brethren, my heart's desire and prayer to God for Israel is, that they might be saved."

Repents:

Rom. 2:4. "But after thy hardness and impenitent heart."

103

Presumes:

Est. 7:5. "Who is he, and where is he that durst presume in his heart to do so?"

Loves:

Matt. 22:37. "Thou shalt love the Lord thy God with all thy heart."

Despises:

2 Sam. 6:16. "And she despised him in her heart."

Double-Hearted:

1 Cor. 12:33. "They were not of double heart."

Double-Minded:

Jas. 1:8. "A double minded man is unstable in all his ways."

Law Written in Heart:

Heb. 8:10. "I will put my laws in their mind, and write them in their hearts."

Law Written in Minds:

Heb. 10:16. "I will put my laws into their hearts, and in their minds will I write them."

Serve God with Spirit:

Rom. 1:9. "For God is my witness, whom I serve with my spirit in the gospel of his Son."

Serve God with Mind:

Rom. 7:25. "With the mind I myself serve the law of God."

Sorrow of Heart:

Neh. 2:2. "Why is thy countenance sad, seeing thou art not sick? This is nothing else but sorrow of heart."

Grieved in Spirit:

Dan. 7:15. "I Daniel was grieved in my spirit."

Obey From the Heart:

Rom. 6:17. "Ye have obeyed from the heart that form of doctrine which was delivered you."

104

The Heart Lives Forever:

Ps. 22:26. "Your heart shall live forever."

From the above quotations you cannot fail to understand what is meant by the word "heart" from the Bible viewpoint.

The heart is the soil in which seed is sown; the products of which are seen in the various characteristics of humanity. There is only one way to open the human heart, *viz.*, by teaching. Jesus said the one who received the word into an "honest and good heart" brought forth fruit. Shallow soil cannot grow a good, large crop. There is no depth, no strength. It is the same with the hearts or minds of people. There are many strong minds—deep soil. Sow the seed, word of God, into such soil, and if they do not allow Satan to steal the word, it will bring forth much fruit. Take the shallow (weak-minded) soil, and while you may plant the seed, word, you do not expect much fruit. There are others with ripe, cultured minds (hearts). You sow the seed and look for the harvest—fruit. But the riches of this world, and cares consequent, absorb all the life principles of the soil and there is no fruit produced, to perfection.

Open the physical heart, and the life blood flows out, the person dies. Just so with the mental heart. Here is a man dead (in ignorance) to the sciences. Teach him the sciences and the former death passes out, giving room for the life principle.

There is growing from the soil (hearts, minds) of men a heavy crop of sin, and because of this crop absorbing all the life principle of the soil, you find such characters dead to all that is morally or spiritually good. You place the better seed, the living seed—

the word of God—into this soil, cultivate it, and you will have a new life developed from the new seed.

The Lord opened Lydia's heart, not her physical heart, but the mental heart. The word of God is the seed—Jesus said so. Paul had the word of God. Lydia was ignorant of God's way of salvation. Paul spoke to her, she heard and understood, and thus her heart (understanding) was opened, and she attended unto the things spoken—obeyed the gospel.

All intellectual life is developed from seed —words. Spiritual life is developed from spiritual seed, *i.e.*, from God's word, which Jesus says is "spirit and life." Jno. 6:63. You can have intellectual growth only by teaching. The life is in the seed. Spiritual life is in God's spiritual seed—his word. Place this in the soil, heart, and let the heart receive it (understand), and life will develop; unless Satan is allowed to take the seed out of the heart. Let us sow the seed of the kingdom. Let the poor benighted one hear, believe, obey and a life will be developed that God will accept and bless.

INSTRUMENTAL MUSIC

Worship in Spirit and in Truth:

"God is a Spirit: and they that worship him must worship him in Spirit and in truth." Jno. 4:24. Worship "in spirit" is to worship sincerely, honestly, conscientiously, believing it to be right. To worship "in truth" is to worship as the "truth" directs. "Thy word is truth." Jno. 17:17. If in our worship we do that which we do not believe to be right it is not "in spirit." If we do things in the worship which we do not find authorized by the Lord, no matter how honest or conscientious we may be, it is not "in truth," and becomes vain worship, and is not by the Lord accepted. Mk. 7:7.

Man Not a Legislator for the Lord:

It is not the province of man to make laws for the Lord, nor to legislate as to the way men shall worship Jehovah.

Must Not Add to the Word of the Lord:

Deut. 4:2. "Ye shall not add to the word which I commanded you, neither shall ye diminish aught from it, that ye may keep the commandments of the Lord your God which I commanded you."

Instrumental Music Not Authorized by Christ:

Christ did not authorize the use of Instrumental Music in the work and worship of the church of Christ, and we must not make additions to his teachings.

Gal. 1:8-9. "Though we, or an angel from heaven, preach any other gospel unto you than that which we have preached unto you, let him be accursed. As I said before, so say I now again, If any man preach any other gospel unto you than that you have received, let him be accursed."

Do All in the Name of the Lord:

Col. 3:17. "Whatsoever ye do in word or deed, do all in the name of the Lord Jesus, giving thanks to God and the Father by him." "In the name of the Lord Jesus" means by the authority of the Lord. People were baptized in the "name of the Lord" (Acts 10:48), *i.e.,* they were baptized by the authority of the Lord. Our knowledge of his

107

authority is found in the New Testament. In matters of worship then he authorizes our words and deeds. "In word" is certainly what we say, what we speak. In "deed" can be nothing more than our acts—the things we do, as contrasted with what we speak. Singing is our word. Playing on an instrument is our deed. But we are to say and do by the authority of Christ. When we sing, it is by his authority, for we are commanded to sing. Playing on an instrument is not commanded, and we cannot, therefore, do it by his authority—in his name—and when one uses it in the worship and work of the church of Christ, he breaks the commandment of the Lord—he sins.

Not of Faith:

Rom. 14:23. "Whatsoever is not of faith is sin." Faith comes by hearing the word of God. Rom. 10:9-17. Since the word of God does not authorize the use of instrumental music in the work and worship of the church of Christ, and faith comes by hearing the word of God, it follows that the use of instrumental music in the church of Christ cannot be "of faith;" and since that which is not of faith is sin, its use is sinful.

Guided Into All Truth:

Jno. 16:13. "When he the Spirit of truth is come, he will guide you into all truth." The apostles were not guided to use the instruments of music in the work and worship of the church of Christ. Since they were guided into "all truth," and were not guided to use instrumental music in the work and worship of the church of Christ, it must follow that such practice does not belong to the system of truth delivered by Christ and into which the Holy Spirit guided the apostles.

All Things to Remembrance:

Jno. 14:26. "But the Comforter, which is the Holy Spirit whom the Father will send in my name, he shall teach you all things, and bring all things to your remembrance, whatsoever I have said unto you." The apostles were not taught to use instrumental music in the worship of the church of Christ, nor did the Holy Spirit bring to their remembrance its use. Such music was not authorized by Christ.

Whole Counsel of God:

Acts 20:27. "I have not shunned to declare unto you all the counsel of God." Paul did not declare instrumental music to be authorized by Jehovah. Those who walk by the counsel of God will not use such music in the church.

Hath Not God:

2 Jno. 9. "Whosoever transgresseth, and abideth not in the doctrine of Christ, hath not God." To "abide in" is to remain in, continue in. To abide in the doctrine of Christ is to remain in, continue in his doctrine. He who uses instrumental music in the work and worship of the church of Christ does not "abide" in the doctrine of Christ—he goes beyond that which is written, beyond that which is authorized by Christ. Such people have not God—they rebel against God.

The Command is to Sing:

Eph. 5:19. "Speaking to one another in psalms, and hymns and spiritual songs, singing and making melody in your hearts to the Lord."

Col. 3:16. "Teaching and admonishing one another in psalms, and hymns and spiritual songs." The command is specific—sing. He who plays an instrument does something the

109

Lord did not command to be done in the church of Christ. He who blows a horn in the worship of the church of Christ does something which the Lord did not command, and does something which makes it impossible for him to obey the command of the Lord while blowing the horn—he cannot sing and blow the horn at the same time. If one man has a right to blow the horn in the worship of the church of Christ, all have the same right; and if all should blow the horn, it would be impossible for them to sing at the same time—it would be impossible for them to do the very thing the Lord commanded, the music the Lord commanded would not be rendered. Instrumental music in churches began with the Catholics.

Melody Unto the Lord:

Eph. 5:19. "Singing and making melody in your hearts to the Lord." By some it is insisted that when we have instrumental music the music is better. I think it will be impossible to find people who do not enjoy good music, and if we are to please the people, I would insist that nothing should be left undone which will contribute to that end. If you will notice carefully the instruction of the Spirit, you will find that we are to "make melody unto the Lord," not to please the people. He who seeks to please the people loses sight of the service which is acceptable to our Creator. "Do I seek to please men? for if yet I please men, I should not be a servant of Christ." Gal. 1:10. He who presumes to add instrumental music to the music the Lord commanded must think the Lord did not know what would please him. My brother, you will please the Lord by doing just what he commanded. When there is a greater

110

desire to please the Lord, and less concern about pleasing the people, there will be more spirituality in the congregation.

Praise—Fruit of Lips:

Heb. 13:15. "Through him let us offer up a sacrifice of praise to God continually, that is, the fruit of our lips which make confession to his name." God cannot be worshiped with machinery, neither with inanimate objects.

Presumptuous Sin:

Ps. 19:13. "Keep back thy servant also from presumptuous sins."

Deut. 18:20. "But the prophet, which shall presume to speak a word in my name, which I have not commanded him to speak, . . . even that prophet shall die."

He who proposes to do, in the name of the Lord, that which the Lord has not commanded, is guilty of a presumptuous sin. The Lord has not commanded the use of instrumental music in the worship of the church of Christ. It follows that he who uses such is guilty of presumptuous sin.

Instrumental Music in Homes; Why Not in Church:

Many good people think that because there is nothing wrong in having instrumental music in our homes, we may also have it in our worship in the church also. He who makes such a contention has not studied as carefully as he should, for to contend that what we may have in our homes we may also have in the church is a fallacious method of reasoning. More, the Lord positively declares that we may have in our homes some things which it is sinful to have in the church. Indeed, the Lord declares we *must* have some things in the home that he positively forbids us having in the church. It is necessary for us to have our necessary food for the sustenance of our physical bodies, and this food we are to have in our homes—at least at some place other than the church. Do you think that because we may and do have our breakfast, lunch and dinner in our homes, we may also have them in the church? Do you know the Lord *positively* forbids such? It is right to have our meals in our homes, but it is *not* right to have the meals in the church worship. The church at Corinth had so far departed from the will of the Master that they made the Lord's Supper a feast, and Paul inquires: "What? have ye not houses to eat and drink in? or despise ye the church of God?" 1 Cor. 11:22. Though it was right for them to partake of their daily food, it was a sin for them to eat their daily food in the church in connection with the worship. It must be apparent to each one that though we may have instrumental music in our homes, such is not a warrant for having it in the worship of the church.

Sing and Have Instrumental Music Too:

Some insist that if they have instrumental music they sing also, and in this way have the music the Lord commanded, and in addition thereto have the instrumental music. I think those who reason so clearly know that instrumental music and vocal music combined is not the music the Lord commanded. If it is right to have more than that which the Lord commands in the worship which he ordained, may we then have on the Lord's table the elements he commanded, and in addition thereto have cakes, pies, bacon, beans, etc. If we are not allowed to make these additions to the elements on

112

the Lord's table, on what ground can we make the additions to the music which the Lord commanded?

Instrumental Music in Old Testament:

By some it is contended that since they had instrumental music in Old Testament times, we may also have it in the church of Christ. It should be remembered that the church of Christ is a New Testament institution, that it did not exist and could not exist before the New Testament became operative. Heb. 9:16-17. In the Old Testament times they offered unto Jehovah animal sacrifices (Ex. 12); shall we, therefore, offer animal sacrifices today in the church of God as sacrifices because they did in the Old Testament times? If it is not right to offer animal sacrifices today, even though they did in Old Testament times, is the fact that they used instrumental music in Old Testament times ground for use of such music today in the church of Christ?

True Worship:

We have two kinds of music—*viz.*, Vocal and Instrumental. Jesus, in conversation with the Samaritan woman, told her that the time was at hand for people to observe "true worship." Jno. 4:23. If "instrumental music" is any part of "true worship," then we must have it to have "true worship."

Christians are "priests" (Rev. 1:6) to offer up "spiritual sacrifices" (1 Pet. 2:5). Since there are only two kinds of music—vocal and instrumental—the question is: Which is "spiritual"? If the instrumental music is the "spiritual" you are forced to admit that man invented it—man, not God, is the author of spiritual worship. If instrumental music is

113

the spiritual, since vocal music differs from the instrumental, it follows that instrumental music is carnal.

The Holy Spirit (after Christ went to heaven) revealed the "perfect law of liberty." In this "perfect law" we are taught the perfect, the "true worship." Anything to be perfect must have all its parts. The apostles did not use instrumental music in the worship, but they had the "true worship." Instrumental music is not necessary to "true worship;" indeed it was a long time after the death of the last apostle before the "true worship" was corrupted by the introduction of instrumental music into the worship.

"Pope Vitalian is related to have first introduced organs into some of the churches of Western Europe, about 670; but the earliest trustworthy account is that of the one sent as a present by the Greek emperor Constantine Copronymus to Pepin, king of the Franks, in 755." (The American Cyclopaedia, Vol. 12, p. 688.)

"The organ is said to have been first introduced into church music by Pope Vitalian I in 666. In 757 a great organ was sent as a present to Pepin by the Byzantine emperor, Constantine Copronymus, and placed in the church of St. Corneille at Compiegne. Soon after Charlemagne's time organs became common." (Chambers Encyclopaedia, Vol. 7, p. 112.)

John Calvin, the illustrious founder of the Presbyterian denomination, says: "Musical instruments in celebrating the praises of God would be no more suitable than the burning of incense, the lighting of lamps, and the restoration of the other shadows of the law. The Papists, therefore, have foolishly borrowed this, as well as many other things, from the Jews. Men who are fond of outward pomp may delight in that noise; but the simplicity which God recommends to us by the apostles is far more pleasing to him. Paul allows us to bless God in the public assembly of the saints, only in a known tongue. (1 Cor. 14:6). . . . What shall we then say of chanting which fills the ears with nothing but an empty sound?" (Com. on Ps. 33).

Theodore Beza, the great Genevan scholar and translator, who was a friend and coadjutor of Calvin, says: "If the apostle justly prohibits the use of unknown tongues in the church, much less would he have tolerated these artificial musical performances which are addressed to the ear alone, and seldom strike the understanding even of the performers themselves." (Girardeau's Ins. Music, p. 166.)

LORD'S SUPPER

Instituted by Christ:

Matt. 26:26-28. "And as they were eating, Jesus took bread, and blessed it, and brake it, and gave it to the disciples, and said, Take, eat; this is my body. And he took the cup, and gave thanks, and gave it to them, saying, Drink ye all of it; for this is my blood of the new testament, which is shed for many for the remission of sins."

Observed in Remembrance of Christ:

1 Cor. 11:24. "And when he had given thanks, he brake it, and said, Take, eat; this

is my body, which is broken for you: this do in remembrance of me."

Monument to the Lord's Death:

1 Cor. 11:26. "For as often as ye eat this bread, and drink this cup, ye do show the Lord's death till he come."

Disciples Observed It:

Acts 20:7. "And upon the first day of the week, when the disciples came together to break bread, Paul preached unto them."

The "first day of the week" came once each week—came each week—that is the time, also how often, the disciples "came together to break bread."

Lord's Table is in the Kingdom:

Lk. 22:29-30. "And I appoint unto you a kingdom, as my Father hath appointed unto me; that ye may eat and drink at my table in my kingdom."

If the church is one thing and the kingdom an institution different therefrom, and the Lord's Supper is a "church ordinance," as some insist, then someone has been guilty of stealing the Lord's table out of the kingdom, where Christ said it would be, and placing it in the church. The Lord's table is in the kingdom, and all who have been born again have a right to eat and drink.

Self-Examination:

1 Cor. 11:28-29. "But let a man examine himself, and so let him eat of that bread, and drink of that cup. For he that eateth and drinketh unworthily, eateth and drinketh damnation to himself, not discerning the Lord's body."

You understand that the Lord's Supper was instituted by Christ himself. It is to be observed by Christians as a manifestation of

116

their faith in Christ who died for them. In observing this institution, Christians also manifest their love for and loyalty to him. The apostle says: "Forsake not the assembling of yourselves," or do not neglect the assembling. They assembled to worship; they observed the communion service when they assembled or came together. They were to come together on the first day of the week. As there can be but one "first" of anything, there can be but one "first" day of any week. An objector may say: It does not mean the first day of every week; but when they assembled to partake of the Lord's Supper, it was on the first day of the week. We will see about this. Writing to the church at Corinth, Paul says: "Every first day of the week, let each of you lay something by." 1 Cor. 16:2. (I give the Greek here.)

Christians are not only to come together to "break bread," but to pray for and with each other, to study the word of God, lift their voices in songs of praise and to give of their means as they may purpose in their hearts. If we are not to assemble the first day of each week, we are not to worship each week. The disciple who fails to meet on the first day of each week fails to worship God; and where you find disciples who fail to worship as God directs, you will find spiritual dearth in that community. Jesus says: "Thou shalt worship the Lord thy God, and him only shalt thou serve" (Matt. 4:10), *i.e.*, thou shalt worship God by serving him. Do not neglect the "assembling of yourselves together." When you come together, tarry (wait) one for another. Being assembled, there should be, must be, prayers, supplications and thanksgiving. From this you cannot fail to learn

117

that when assembled it was to worship, and we can worship only by doing God's will—by serving God. If we fail to come together, we fail to serve God; and if we fail to serve God, we do not worship him. Jesus says: "If a man love me, he will keep my words." Jno. 14:23. If you do not assemble as the Lord directs, it is because you do not love the Lord.

When the disciples assemble on the first day of the week, there is something eaten. If we fail to take food for the physical man, body, we will perish—die. So in the life of God's children; if they fail to eat the spiritual food, they dwindle away—die.

"Not forsaking the assembling of ourselves together, as the manner of some is; but exhorting one another: and so much the more, as ye see the day approaching." Heb. 10:25. You should not only assemble, but as you see the day approaching, you should exhort others to assemble. The "day approaching." What day? Certainly the day on which they "assembled," which was the first day of the week. In the days of Paul some were failing to "assemble," and so it is now. You should not be remiss in the discharge of your duty. To fail to serve the Lord in his appointed way is certain proof of your lack of love for him, and means that in the end you will be rejected. Serve the Lord; he will give you blessings here, and a home beyond this lapsed state.

MIRACLES OF CHRIST

Blind men (two) healed. Matt. 9:27-31.

Blind man healed. Mk. 8:22-26.

Blind and dumb healed. Matt. 12:22; Lk. 11:14.

118

Bartimeus healed. Matt. 20:30-34; Mk. 10:46-52; Lk. 18:35-43.

Born blind, healed. Jno. 9:1-7.

Christ passed unseen. Lk. 4:30.

Centurion's servant healed. Matt. 8:5-13; Lk. 7:1-10.

Dumb healed. Mk. 9:14-27.

Deaf and dumb healed. Mk. 7:31-37.

Dropsy healed. Lk. 14:1-4.

Demoniac in synagogue cured. Mk. 1:23-26; Lk. 4:33-35.

Demoniac child cured. Matt. 17:14-18; Mk. 9:17-29; Lk. 9:38-42.

Daughter of Syrophenician healed. Matt. 15:21-28; Mk. 7:24-30.

Devils enter swine. Matt. 8:28-34; Mk. 5:1-15; Lk. 8:27-35.

Draught of fishes. Lk. 5:1-11.

Draught of fishes. Jno. 21:1-11.

Fish—money in its mouth. Matt. 17:24-27.

Feeding four thousand. Matt. 15:32-38; Mk. 8:1-8.

Feeding five thousand. Matt. 14:19-20; Mk. 6:35-44; Lk. 9:12-17; Jno. 6:5-13.

Fig tree cursed. Matt. 21:18-22; Mk. 11:12-14.

Impotent man at Bethsaida healed. Jno. 5:1-9.

Jairus' daughter raised. Matt. 9:23-25; Mk. 5:38-42; Lk. 8:49-56.

Lazarus raised. Jno. 11:43-44.

Lepers, ten healed. Lk. 17:11-19.

Leper. Matt. 8:2-3; Mk. 1:40-42; Lk. 5:12-13.

Malchus' ear healed. Lk. 22:50-51.

Nobleman's son.

Peter's mother-in-law. Matt. 8:14-15; Mk. 1:30-31; Lk. 4:38-39.

Palsy cured. Mk. 2:3-12; Lk. 5:18-26.

Storm at sea. Matt. 8:26; Mk. 4:37-39; Lk. 8:22-24.

Widow's son raised. Lk. 7:11-15.

Woman with infirmity cured. Lk. 13:11-13.

Water turned into wine. Jno. 2:1-11.

Woman with issue of blood. Matt. 9:20-22; Mk. 5:20-29; Lk. 8:43-48.

Withered hand cured. Matt. 12:10-13; Mk. 3:1-5; Lk. 6:6-10.

Walking on the sea. Matt. 14:25; Mk. 6:48-51; Jno. 6:19-21.

The miracles performed by our Savior were greatly the fulfillment of prophetic statements concerning Christ. In order to prove himself the Messiah of prophecy, he must do the things the prophets foretold he would. Hence, "Lo, I come . . . to do thy will, O God." The Jews had no excuse for not believing him—they had the oracles of God.

Though the miracles of Christ were the fulfilment of prophecy, the Jews rejected him, and in so doing they rejected Moses, for Jesus says: "He testified of me." Hence, when the Jews rejected Christ they rejected God, the prophets and Moses. The apostles of Christ performed many miracles; the object of these miracles was twofold, viz., to confirm the word spoken and to convince the people that they were sent from God with the message. The word has been confirmed and sealed by the oath of heaven and blood of Christ. There is nothing that could be said or done to confirm the word of God that has not been said and done, and is a matter of record. Hence, we no longer have miracles. We have the record and should believe it.

_____

NATURE OF MAN

Body, Soul and Spirit:
1 Thess. 5:23. "I pray God your whole spirit, and soul, and body, be preserved blameless unto the coming of our Lord Jesus Christ."

Offspring of God:
Acts 17:29. "Forasmuch then as we are the offspring of God."

Father of Flesh and Spirit Contrasted:
Heb. 12:9. "Furthermore we have had fathers of our flesh which corrected us, and we gave them reverence: shall we not much rather be in subjection unto the Father of spirits and live?"

Spirit in Man:
Dan. 7:15. "I Daniel was grieved in my spirit in the midst of my body."

The Spirit Knows:
1 Cor. 2:11. "For what man knoweth the things of a man, save the spirit of man which is in him?"

The Spirit Lives:
Isa. 38:16. "In all these things is the life of my spirit."

The Body Dies:
Jas. 2:26. "For the body without the spirit is dead."

Spirit Returns to God:
Eccl. 12:7. "Then shall the dust return to the earth as it was; and the spirit shall return unto God who gave it."

Receive My Spirit:

Lk. 23:46. "And when Jesus had cried with a loud voice, he said, Father, into thy hands I commend my spirit."

We Fly Away:

Ps. 90:10. "The days of our years are three-score years and ten; and if by reason of strength they be fourscore years, yet is their strength labor and sorrow; for it is soon cut off, and we fly away."

Depart and Be With Christ

Phil. 1:21-24. "For me to live is Christ, and to die is gain. But if I live in the flesh, this is the fruit of my labor: yet what I shall choose I wot not. For I am in a strait betwixt two, having a desire to depart, and to be with Christ; which is far better: nevertheless, to abide in the flesh is more needful for you."

Absent From Body—Present With the Lord:

2 Cor. 5:6-8. "Therefore we are always confident, knowing that, whilst we are at home in the body, we are absent from the Lord (for we walk by faith, not by sight): we are confident, I say, and willing rather to be absent from the body, and to be present with the Lord."

Put Off the Tabernacle—Body:

2 Pet. 1:13-14. "Yea, I think it meet, as long as I am in this tabernacle, to stir you up by putting you in remembrance; knowing that shortly I must put off this my tabernacle, even as our Lord Jesus Christ hath showed me."

Man Can Kill Body Only:

Lk. 12:4-5. "And I say unto you, my friends, Be not afraid of them that kill the body, and after that have no more that they can do. But I forewarn you whom ye shall fear: Fear him, which after he hath killed hath power to cast into hell."

Live Forever:

Psa. 22:26. "The meek shall eat and be satisfied: they shall praise the Lord that seek him: your heart shall live forever."

No Death:

Prov. 12:28. "In the way of righteousness is life; and in the pathway thereof there is no death."

Never Die:

Jno 11:26. "Whosoever liveth, and believeth in me, shall never die. Believest thou this?" The body of saint and sinner does die, but one who believes in Christ is not to die—then it is not the body that is contemplated.

Never See Death:

Jno. 8:51-52. "Verily, verily, I say unto you, if a man keep my sayings, he shall never see death. Then said the Jews unto him, now we know thou hast a devil. Abraham is dead, and the prophets; and thou sayest, If a man keep my sayings, he shall never taste of death." Certainly Jesus knew that Abraham was dead, if the body is all there is contemplated. But Abraham lived. Those who say a man dies, body, soul and spirit, accuse Christ of having a devil, as did the people above.

The God of Abraham—Not God of Dead:

Lk. 20:39. "Now that the dead are raised, even Moses showed at the bush, when he called the Lord the God of Abraham, and the God of Isaac, and the God of Jacob. For he is not a God of the dead, but of the living: for all live unto him." When Moses made the above statement, Abraham's body had been buried. (1) God is not God of the dead. (2) God is God

123

of Abraham. (3) Therefore Abraham lived unto God—his body was dead, but his spirit was not.

If the Spirit in Man is Nothing but His Breath, What About the Following:

Lev. 20:27. "A man also or a woman that hath a familiar spirit." Does this mean a "familiar breath"?

Jno. 13:21. "When Jesus had thus said, he was troubled in spirit." Does this mean that he had "asthma, or a difficulty in breathing"?

2 Cor. 7:1. "Having therefore these promises, dearly beloved, let us cleanse ourselves from all filthiness of the flesh and spirit." Filthiness of the spirit—does that mean that we must use perfumed tooth powders so our breath will not be foul?

1 Pet. 3:4. "But let it be the hidden man of the heart, in that which is not corruptible, even the ornament of a meek and quiet spirit." Meek and quiet spirit. That is that one must not snore, eh?

If Death Means "Ceasing to Be," Read the Following:

Matt. 8:22. "But Jesus said unto him, Follow me; and let the dead bury their dead" —that is, let those who "cease to be" bury those who "cease to be."

1 Tim. 5:6. "But she that liveth in pleasure is dead while she liveth"—that is, she is living, but does not exist.

If it was not for the many foolish theories advocated, and the "cunning craftiness, whereby they lie in wait to deceive," it would not be necessary to notice the question of the "nature of man." There are men who teach (and I presume they believe) that man is

124

"wholly mortal." Webster defines mortal: "Subject to death." There is nothing subject to death and decay, but matter. If man is wholly subject to death, then man is all matter. Those who hold to the position that man is "wholly mortal" certainly do not consider the consequences of such a position. I boldly affirm: If man is wholly mortal—all matter—he cannot be an intellectual being. Matter alone cannot be intelligent or moral. You cannot predicate intellectuality or morality of matter. What? Muscle, blood and bone think? Why cannot a dead man think? He has all the muscle, blood and bone he possessed before death. He is just as much matter now as before his death. Do you say that he is dead, and for that reason he cannot think? What has that to do with it? If the air he breathed is the life of the body, you know the air has no intelligence; besides, you can pump the dead body full of air, and it will neither think nor live. Do you say the spirit has left the body, and he is dead? Just so. Is the spirit any part of the man? Materialists say "no." Why? Because Jesus says: "A spirit hath not flesh and bones." Lk. 24:39. They insist that man is "wholly mortal"— their man is flesh, bone and blood. But "spirit" is not "flesh and bones," and cannot be any part of the man of the Materialist. But since the spirit is not flesh and bone, nor matter, it is not subject to death and decay. The spirit being no part of the man the Materialists talk about, you cannot fail to see that though the spirit leaves the body, the whole man of the Materialist is left, for all the flesh, bone—all the mortal part—is there. While the spirit was in the body there was just that much more than the man of the

125

Materialist—the spirit is no part of the man, they say. Take the spirit from the man the Materialist talks about, and you still have the man left; but he knows nothing, feels nothing, sees nothing. In short, the man as defined by Materialists is subject to two laws only, *viz.*, gravity and decomposition. Neither intellectuality, morality nor spirituality are attributes of matter. If you say I am mistaken about this matter (I know I am not), then Materialists are forced to the position that intellectuality, morality and spirituality are attributes of matter, and it follows, the more matter the more intellectuality. My, but how intelligent would an elephant be, according to the theory of the Materialists!

"What man knoweth the things of a man, save the spirit of man which is in him?" 1 Cor. 2:11. Note: The man the Materialist talks about knows not one thing—not one! They say the spirit is no part of the man. But Paul says the spirit in man knows the things of man, and for man. A man is in a house; he knows the things of the house, but the house does not know anything. Materialists make the man the house, and the spirit in the man no part of the man. According to them, the spirit is no more a part of the man than the man in the house is a part of the house. Man can leave the house, and you have the house —the complete house—left; just so, they declare, the spirit can leave the body, and you have the entire man left. The house knows nothing, neither does the thing they call man, and never did.

The man the Materialists talk about can neither be rewarded nor punished. Why? Because he is inert matter. There cannot be punishment in the absence of consciousness, and what they call man is not conscious, and never was; and for that reason cannot be punished or rewarded.

What is "soul"? Those who teach that man is "wholly mortal" say: Soul is a being—a person, the mortal body. That is, with them, body is man, man is soul, and soul is body. God says: "The soul that sinneth, it shall die." Sin stands as the cause, death the effect. If the soul never sinned, it would never die. If it did, you would have an effect without a cause. As the soul (body) must sin, before it can die (according to the Materialist), I am a bit anxious to know why the infant dies. Do you say they are sinners? Then why did Christ die? Was he a sinner?

As sin stands as the cause, and death the effect, it follows that should you remove the cause—sin—man could not die. Why? Simply because you have removed the cause and there is nothing to produce the effect. Should a man prove to be as good as the Holiness claim to be—live above sin—he would never die, per the Materialists' position on the nature of man. If God pardons a man, he cannot die, till he sins, per the doctrine of the Materialists. But all die, but it is the "soul that sinneth" that dies; it follows then that all die sinners; and if any one is in heaven they are there as sinners, or they are pardoned after they die. I have shown that man is composed of body, soul and spirit. Reader, turn from the theories of men; hear, learn and obey the truth—be faithful till death, and you will receive the crown of life.

(For a full discussion of the "Nature of Man," see the *Nichol-Bradley Debate.*)

OPERATION OF THE SPIRIT.

Convinces of Sin:

Jno. 16:8. "And when he is come, he will reprove [convince] the world of sin." It is not a question that the Spirit is to convince of sin, but how does it do this work?

1 Tim. 1:15. Paul declares that he was a sinner, and now the question: how did he know that he was a sinner? Let him answer:

Rom. 3:20. "By the law is the knowledge of sin." While the Spirit is to convince of sin, the knowledge of sin came by the law. Certainly the Spirit convinced him of sin by the law.

There are so many theories regarding the work of the Spirit, I wish to add a few words.

Many people seem to think the Holy Spirit exercises a power in conviction and conversion, independent of any and all agencies. They pray for God to send "converting power." Evidently they do not believe what David said about conversion, *viz.,* "The law of the Lord is perfect, converting the soul." Ps. 19:7. Paul says: "Lest they should see with their eyes, hear with their ears, and understand with their hearts, and should be converted, and I should heal them." Acts 28:27. As the "law of the Lord" converts, and man is to "see, hear and understand" to be converted; if the Spirit converts he does so by giving the law by which man is converted. God pardons the converted. But Paul says: "The law of the Spirit of life in Christ Jesus hath made me free from the law of sin and death." Rom. 8:2. As the "law of the Spirit" made Paul free, and man must be converted before God pardons him, and the "law of the Lord" converts the soul, I am sure the "law of the Spirit" and the "law of the Lord" which converts the soul are the same. Why? God saves (heals) the converted; but the "law of the Lord" converts. Therefore God brings man to salvation by his law. Paul declares the "law of the Spirit" made him free. Then he was brought to salvation by the "law of the Spirit." As man is not saved till converted, and the "law of the Lord" converts, the law by which man is converted and brought to salvation is the "law of the Spirit."

Peter says the gospel was preached—"by them that have preached the gospel unto you with the Holy Ghost sent down from heaven." 1 Pet. 1:12. The Holy Spirit preached the gospel. The gospel is the power of God unto salvation. Rom. 1:16. God saves the converted. Therefore, the gospel preached by the Spirit sent down from heaven is the means used by the Spirit to convert.

Law is a rule of action. Not for God; God never ordained a law for himself—he ordains law for men. As the "law of the Lord" converts, and law is a rule of action, then God has ordained a law, in obedience to which man is converted, and God pardons him. The Spirit is not law any more than God is law. As the "law of the Lord" converts and the Holy Spirit is not law, but the speaker of the law, then the only way the Spirit converts is to speak the "law of the Lord" by which you are converted.

More than four hundred years before the birth of Christ, the prophet said: "Yet many years didst thou forbear them, and testified against them by thy Spirit in thy prophets." Neh. 9:30. God rebuked them by his Spirit in the prophets, telling them what to do. In his way the Spirit regulates the lives of men.

If the Spirit comes directly from God to convert sinners, the Bible is not true—unless the Spirit comes to the sinner to bring the "law of the Lord," the converting power. If it is necessary for the Spirit to bring the "law of the Lord," then the Bible does not contain the "law of the Lord." But the Bible contains the "law of the Lord," and if the Spirit must come directly from God to convert, then the Bible is not true, for it says: "The law of the Lord is perfect, converting the soul."

One must "see, hear and understand" to be converted. Jesus says the one "having heard the word, keep it, and bring forth fruit with patience." Lk. 8:15. If man is converted by the Spirit, independent of the word of God, and saved when converted, then he is saved without faith. For faith comes by hearing the word of God. Rom. 10:17. But if the Spirit converts him and enables him to believe, then he had to be converted before he could believe, and as God saves the converted, it follows that he was saved before he could believe. If it is said that the Spirit in his power is necessary to enable man to believe that he might be saved, then the law, the converting power, can have no effect on the sinner to convert him till the Spirit operates on the sinner. If this position be true, the Spirit itself does not convert the sinner, but operates on the sinner to enable him to believe. If this be true, then a sinner cannot believe without this operation, and as he cannot be saved till he believes, then he cannot be saved till the Spirit operates on him. The matter stands thus: The Spirit operates on the sinner to enable him to believe. All the Spirit operates on will believe (if this is denied, then the Spirit failed in its work), and all who believe will be saved. Then if man is lost, it is because God withholds the power which would enable him to believe and be saved, and then sends him to hell for not believing. Per the theory: Man can't believe till God sends him the enabling power of the Spirit; but God does not send the power to all men by which they are enabled to believe, and then sends them to hell for not believing. Reader, do you believe that God is so unjust? I beg you, accept the truth; the Spirit has given the word—the law of God. You are to believe his word, obey him, God saves you.

God does not teach that the Spirit is the Savior of men. He teaches by the Spirit that Christ is the Savior. The Spirit did not die for you. Jesus did. The Spirit testifies to this fact. The Spirit did not shed blood for you— he did not have blood to shed. "The blood of Jesus Christ his Son cleanseth us from all sin." 1 Jno. 1:7. As the blood of Christ cleanseth you from all sin, there is not a sin the Spirit cleanseth you from. The Spirit does teach how you may be cleansed by the blood of Christ—in the Bible you find just what to do, that you may honor Christ and be saved by his blood.

Christ says: "I am the way, the truth, and the life: no man cometh unto the Father but by me." Jno. 14:6. You do not reach the Father by the Spirit, but the Spirit tells you how to reach the Father by Christ—the way, the only way. The Spirit is not God's mediator, and you can reach—approach— God only by mediation. You cannot approach God through the Spirit, for there is "one mediator between God and man, the man

Christ Jesus." 1 Tim. 2:5. The Spirit tells how to reach God through the only mediator. Let your faith rest in what the Spirit has taught regarding Christ the Savior. Lovingly obey him and be saved.

Word and Spirit

Quickened by the Spirit:

Jno. 6:63. "It is the Spirit that quickeneth; the flesh profiteth nothing: the words that I speak unto you, they are spirit, and they are life."

Ps. 119:50. "Thy word hath quickened me."

Sanctified by the Spirit:

1 Cor. 6:11. "But ye are sanctified, but ye are justified in the name of the Lord Jesus, and by the Spirit of our God."

Sanctified by the Word:

Jno. 17:17. "Sanctify them through thy truth: thy word is truth."

To Whom is the Spirit Given?

To Believers:

Jno. 7:39. "But this spake he of the Spirit, which they that believe on him should receive."

Through Faith:

Gal. 3:14. "That we might receive the promise of the Spirit through faith."

To Them That Obey God:

Acts 5:32. "And we are witnesses of these things; and so is also the Holy Ghost, whom God hath given to them that obey him."

To Sons of God:

Gal. 4:6. "And because ye are sons, God hath sent forth the Spirit of his Son into your hearts, crying, Abba, Father."

The World Can't Receive It:

Jno. 14:16-17. "And I will pray the Father, and he shall give you another Comforter, that he may abide with you forever; even the Spirit of truth; whom the world cannot receive."

Why Did the Spirit Fall In Cornelius?

Not to Save Him:

Acts 11:13-14. "And he [Cornelius] showed us how he had seen an angel in his house, which stood and said unto him, Send men to Joppa, and call for Simon, whose surname is Peter; who shall tell thee words, whereby thou and all thy house shall be saved."

Not to Purify His Heart:

Acts 15:9. "And put no difference between us and them, purifying their hearts by faith."

Not to Give Faith:

Acts 15:7. "And when there had been much disputing, Peter rose up, and said unto them, Men and brethren, ye know how that a good while ago God made choice among us, that the Gentiles by my mouth should hear the word of the gospel, and believe."

Not to Purify Soul:

1 Pet. 1:22. "Seeing ye have purified your souls in obeying the truth."

Not to Convert:

Ps. 19:7. "The law of the Lord is perfect, converting the soul."

Not to Sanctify:

Jno. 17:17. "Sanctify them through thy truth, thy word is truth."

Not to Give Remission of Sins:

Acts 10:43. "To him give all the prophets witness, that through his name whosoever believeth in him shall receive the remission of sins."

Not to Produce the New Birth:

1 Pet. 1:23. "Being born again, not of corruptible seed, but of incorruptible, by the word of God, which liveth and abideth forever." Note—To be born of the "word" is to be born of the "Spirit," for (Jno. 6:63), "The words I speak unto you, they are Spirit and they are life." If you say "word" means "the Lord," then (2 Cor. 3:17): "Now the Lord is that Spirit;" so that to be born of the "word" is to be born of the "spirit."

Note—Before the conversion of Cornelius the apostles had preached only to their own nation—the Jews. Peter was convinced by the miracle (Acts 11:1-8) that he should go to the Gentiles. When he started, he took with him six Jewish brethren (Acts 11:12-18), but these six were not convinced that the gospel should be preached to the Gentiles. When they reached the house of Cornelius, the Spirit was poured out on Cornelius and those of his house, and in this way were the Jews— the six Jews that Peter took with him—convinced that the gospel should be preached to the Gentiles, and to convince them was the purpose of the outpouring of the Spirit at the house of Cornelius.

Though I have given you the above scripture relative to the conversion of Cornelius, I wish to add a few thoughts.

To the disciples Jesus said: The Spirit "will guide you into all truth," (Jno. 16:13), or reveal all truth to you. Cornelius did not receive the Spirit for that purpose; if he did, there was no necessity for Peter preaching the truth to him—the Spirit could have done that independent of the preaching by Peter. Peter said: "God made choice among us, that the Gentiles by my mouth should hear the word of the gospel, and believe." Acts 15:7. Then the Spirit did not fall on Cornelius to give him faith; nor was it to make a witness of him; for one had to see Jesus after he was raised from the dead to be a witness. After his resurrection God "showed him openly; not to all the people, but unto witnesses chosen before of God, even to us, who did eat and drink with him after he rose from the dead." Acts 10:41. It was not to reveal to him the truth, for that was a matter of revelation, for some eight years. It is evident to my mind that when Jesus said, "whom the world cannot receive," he was talking of the world not receiving the Spirit in the sense and for the purpose it was given to the disciples. We will see about this later. Some entertain the view that the sinner must receive the baptism of the Spirit before they can be saved, and that the outpouring of the Spirit at the house of Cornelius was a baptism and for that purpose. If this be true, there could be no purpose in Peter going to Cornelius.

Was Cornelius saved before Peter entered his house? "No;" for the angel said (Acts 10:6) Peter would tell him what to do. If saved before Peter spoke to him, he was saved before doing what he "ought to do." But Peter was to tell Cornelius words whereby he could be saved: "Who shall tell thee words, whereby thou and thy house shall be saved." Acts 11:14. If he was saved before Peter spoke to him, he was saved without faith, for he was to hear the gospel from Peter, and believe. Acts 15:7. As faith comes by hearing the word of God (Rom. 10:17), and he did not hear the word till Peter preached to him, then I am certain if he was saved before Peter went to him, he was saved without faith. No only so, but he was saved without the "power of God," for he was to hear the gospel from Peter, and the gospel is the power of God unto salvation. Rom. 1:16. This is sufficient to show that he was not saved at the time Peter entered his house.

I will now show what the outpouring of the Spirit was not for:

It was not to teach him what to do. Peter was to do that. Acts 10:6.

It was not to give him faith. Faith was to come by hearing words from Peter. Acts 15:7. Then it was not to save him, for he could not be saved without faith, and faith comes by hearing God's word, and the angel and Peter declared he was to hear that word from Peter. Another reason I know the outpouring of the Spirit was not to save him: he had to be saved through faith, and by the power of God. The gospel being the power of God unto salvation, and the outpouring of the Spirit not being the gospel, I know it is not the power of God unto salvation, nor any part of said power.

The apostles preached the gospel. Jesus prayed for all who believe on him through their word. Jno. 17:20. As they preached the gospel, and Jesus prayed for all who believe through their word, he prayed for all who believe through the gospel. As man is saved by faith, and faith comes by hearing the word of God, and the outpouring of the Spirit is not words, I know that faith and the salvation consequent is not by the outpouring of the Spirit. I know the outpouring of the Spirit was not to convert Cornelius, for "the law of the Lord is perfect, converting the soul." Cornelius had to be converted before God would save him. Acts 28:27. The "law of the Lord" converts the soul. The outpouring of the Spirit is not the "law of the Lord;" therefore I know outpouring of the Spirit was not to convert him. As the "law of the Lord" converts, and Cornelius had to be converted before God would save him, and Peter was to tell him "words whereby" he and his house could be saved, and as Peter preached the gospel, I am certain the "gospel" is the "law of the Lord" by which Cornelius was converted—saved.

Peter said: "Cornelius, God is no respecter of persons; but in every nation he that feareth him, and worketh righteousness, is accepted with him." Acts 10:34-35. Cornelius feared God before Peter went to him (Acts 10:2), but he had not "worked righteousness." How do I know? The righteousness of God is in the gospel. Rom. 1:17. Righteousness of God is the commandments of God. Ps. 119:172. He was to hear the word of the gospel from Peter's mouth; Peter was to tell him what to do to be saved; but Peter tells him he must work righteousness before God will accept him. As righteousness is in the gospel, and the commandments of God is righteousness, then he tells him that he must obey the gospel before he can be saved—before God will accept him. Whatever Peter commanded him was a command of the gospel, for he preached the gospel. As the angel told him Peter would tell him words whereby he should be saved, and Peter tells him he must work righteousness to be saved; whatever Peter commands him to do was a work of righteousness necessary to salvation. But Peter commanded him to be baptized in the name of the Lord. Then he had to do that before the Lord would accept him.

What was the outpouring of the Spirit for? I answer: To convince Peter and the six Jews with him that the Gentiles were to receive the gospel and salvation through Christ. The Jews did not believe this, hence the miracle. Peter now understands what the Lord meant when he said: "When thou art converted, strengthen thy brethren" (Lk. 22:32), and says: "Brethren, ye know how that a good while ago God made choice among us, that the Gentiles by my mouth should hear the word of the gospel, and believe." Peter is now converted to the fact that the Gentiles are to have the gospel blessing as well as the Jews; and proceeded to strengthen the brethren. When he went to Jerusalem, from the house of Cornelius, his brethren inquired as to his action in going to the Gentiles. Peter rehearsed the entire matter. When they heard his defense, "they held their peace, and glorified God, saying, Then hath God also to the Gentiles granted repentance unto life." Acts 11:18. Peter strengthened his brethren. When trouble came up over the circumcision of the Gentiles, Peter is to the front, and his speech is final. The outpouring of the Spirit on Cornelius and his household was to convince Peter and through him the Jewish brotherhood that the Gentiles were to be accepted in the gospel.

PARABLES.

Barren Fig Tree. Lk. 13:6-9.

Blade—Ear—Full-grown Corn. Mk. 4:26-29.

Candle Under Bushel. Matt. 5:15; Mk. 4:31; Lk. 8:16; 11:33.

Fig Tree—All Trees. Matt. 24:32-33; Mk. 13:28-29; Lk. 21:29-32.

Goodly Pearl. Matt. 13:45-46.

Good Samaritan. Lk. 10:30-35.

Great Supper. Lk. 14:16-34.

House on Rock and Sand. Matt. 7:24-27; Lk. 6:47-49.

Householder. Mk. 13:34.

Importuned Friend. Lk. 11:5-8.

Laborers in Vineyard. Matt. 20:1-16.

Leaven. Matt. 13:33; Lk. 13:20-21.

Lost Sheep. Matt. 18:12-13; Lk. 15:4-6.

Marriage of King's Son. Matt. 22:2-14.

Mustard Seed. Matt. 13:31-32; Mk. 4:30-31; Lk. 13:18-19.

Net. Matt. 13:47-48.

New Cloth—Old Garments. Matt. 9:16; Mk. 2:21; Lk. 5:36.

New Wine—Old Bottles. Matt. 9:17; Mk. 2:22; Lk. 5:37-38.

Nobleman—Far Country. Lk. 19:12-27.

Piece of Money—Lost, Found. Lk. 15:8-10.

Prodigal Son. Lk. 15:11-32.

Pharisee and Publican. Lk. 18:10-14.

Rich Fool. Lk. 12:16-20.

Rich Man and Lazarus. Lk. 16:19-31. (This is often spoken of as a parable, but am fully persuaded that it is not.)

Sheep and Goats. Matt. 25:31-46.

Sower. Matt. 13:3-8; Mk. 4:3-8; Lk. 8:5-8.

Servants Watching. Lk. 12:25-40.

A parable is a comparison, a similitude. In the parables of Jesus, he has taught lessons concerning his kingdom, the preparations for and growth and development of the same. By parables he illustrated every phase of human life, often rebuking the people by comparisons; he never failed to point out the right.

In the parables illustrative of his future kingdom, he would explain to his disciples the lesson taught. In the parables of the kingdom, you will find two leading thoughts —viz., preparation and futurity. Showing the importance of his kingdom, he says: "The kingdom of heaven is like a treasure hid in a field; . . . when the man hath found, he sells all he hath and buyeth that field." The treasures, or blessings of God, are in the kingdom; but man must give up all sinful practices before he can come into possession of the blessings. He did not teach the world the meaning of the parables concerning the kingdom and the blessings to be man's therein—the disciples were to teach the law of induction into the kingdom, when it was established. By parables he was teaching the importance of the kingdom, and the necessity of their reformation before they could become subjects of the same.

In parables he rebuked the Jews for their sinful lives, especially for their hypocrisy. They pretended to be zealous of the law, while they were violating every principle of the same.

To the rich Pharisees he gave the parable (?) of the rich man and Lazarus. In this he rebuked the rich man for not caring for his poor brethren, who were not able to help themselves. It was the world-loving rich that persecuted him and rejected his teachings. The poor heard him gladly. The end comes; both die, the rich man left all his earthly possessions; the character he had, God rejected, and now he is homeless, friendless and miserable. He was not rejected because of his wealth, but because of his lack of compassion and care for those about him that he could have blessed with his wealth—he neglected the poor. Had he used his means as God directs, he would have been blessed in time and been with God in eternity. This warns us. The poor heard Jesus, and though he died poor, he died rich. He had laid up treasures in heaven. Though poor here, over yonder you may have plenty. The rich here may be poor over yonder.

Another lesson taught in this parable— viz.: There is no opportunity to reform after death. The poor did not want a chance, and the rich man could not have one. While living here is the time to lay up treasures in heaven.

The final lesson: The one who shows no pity here and rejects Christ will spend eternity in torment.

PRAYER

Pray to Whom:

Col. 1:3. "We give thanks to God and the Father of our Lord Jesus Christ, praying always for you."

Through Whom:

Rom. 1:8. "I thank God through Jesus Christ for you all." Col. 3:17. "And whatsoever ye do in word or deed, do all in the name of the Lord Jesus, giving thanks to God and the Father by him."

Pray, How Often:

Rom. 12:12. "Rejoicing in hope; patient in tribulation; continuing instant in prayer."

Why Pray:

Heb. 4:16. "Let us therefore come boldly unto the throne of grace, that we may obtain mercy, and find grace to help in time of need."

Pray for Whom.

1 Tim. 2:1-2. "I exhort therefore, that, first of all, supplications, prayers, intercessions, and giving of thanks be made for all men; for kings, and for all that are in authority; that we may lead a quiet and peaceable life in all godliness and honesty."

Forgive When You Pray:

Mk. 11:25-26. "And when ye stand praying, forgive, if ye have aught against any: that your Father also which is in heaven may forgive you your trespasses. But if ye do not forgive, neither will your Father which is in heaven forgive your trespasses."

Ask in Faith:

Jas. 1:6-7. "Ask in faith, nothing wavering. For he that wavereth is like a wave of the sea driven with the wind and tossed. for let not that man think that he shall receive anything of the Lord."

Ask According to His Will:

1 Jno. 5:14-15. "This is the confidence we have in him, that, if we ask anything according to his will, he heareth us: and if we know that he hear us, whatsoever we ask we know that we have the petitions that we desire of him."

Received, if Keep Commandments:

1 Jno. 3:22. "And whatsoever we ask, we receive of him, because we keep his commandments, and do those things that are pleasing in his sight."

Lifting Up Holy Hands:

1 Tim. 2:8. "I will therefore that men pray everywhere, lifting up holy hands, without wrath and doubtings."

Ears Open to Righteous:

Ps. 34:15. "For the eyes of the Lord are over the righteous, and his ears are open unto their cries."

Eyes Over Righteous:

1 Pet. 3:12. "For the eyes of the Lord are over the righteous, and his ears are open unto their prayers: but the face of the Lord is against them that do evil."

Ask and Receive Not:

Jas. 4:3. "Ye ask, and receive not, because ye ask amiss, that ye may consume it upon your lusts."

Pray for Each Other:

2 Thess. 3:1-2. "Finally, brethren, pray for us, that the word of the Lord may have free course, and be glorified, even as it is with

you: and that we may be delivered from unreasonable men."

God Will Not Hear.

God Hears Not Sinners:

Jno. 9:31. "Now we know that God heareth not sinners." How did the blind man know that God did not hear sinners? Note the following quotations, and you will learn how the blind man knew:

Far From the Wicked:

Prov. 15:29. "The Lord is far from the wicked: but he heareth the prayers of the righteous."

Sacrifice of Wicked an Abomination:

Prov. 15:8. "The sacrifice of the wicked is an abomination to the Lord: but the prayer of the upright is his delight."

Prayer An Abomination:

Prov. 28:9. "He that turneth away his ear from hearing the law, even his prayer shall be an abomination."

Face Against Evildoers:

Psa. 34:16. "The face of the Lord is against them that do evil."

Regard Iniquity—Will Not Hear:

Ps. 66:18. "If I regard iniquity in my heart, the Lord will not hear me."

Must Ask in Faith:

God will not hear a prayer, unless the one praying has faith. But if one is saved the moment he has "faith," how can such a man pray for salvation?

For What Should the Sinner Pray?

Not for God to Love Him:

Jno. 3:16. "For God so loved the world, that he gave his only begotten Son, that whosoever believeth in him should not perish."

Not for Light, Because:

Ps. 119:130. "The entrance of Thy word giveth light."

Not for Understanding, Because:

Ps. 119:130. "The entrance of thy word giveth light; it giveth understanding unto the simple."

Not for the Spirit, Because:

Jno. 14:16-17. "And I will pray the Father, and he shall give you another Comforter, that he may abide with you forever; even the Spirit of truth; whom the world cannot receive."

Not for Christ to Come Unto Him, Because:

Matt. 11:28. "Come unto me, all ye that labor and are heavy laden, and I will give you rest."

Not for God to be Reconciled to Him, Because:

2 Cor. 5:20. "Now then we are ambassadors for Christ, as though God did beseech you by us: we pray you in Christ's stead, be ye reconciled to God."

Not for Grace:

Titus 2:11. "For the grace of God that bringeth salvation hath appeared to all men."

Not for Pardon:

Isa. 55:7. "Let the wicked forsake his way, and the unrighteous man his thoughts: and let him return unto the Lord, and he will have mercy upon him, and to our God, for he will abundantly pardon."

Not for Conversion, Because:

Psa. 19:7. "The law of the Lord is perfect, converting the soul."

Not for Faith, Because:

Rom. 10:17. "So then faith cometh by hearing, and hearing by the word of God."

Not for Salvation:

Acts 11:14. "Who shall tell thee words whereby thou and all thy house shall be saved." Jas. 1:21. "Wherefore laying aside all filthiness and superfluity of naughtiness receive with meekness the engrafted word, which is able to save your souls." Mk. 16:16. "He that believeth and is baptized shall be saved."

Not for the New Birth:

1 Pet. 1:22-23. "Seeing ye have purified your souls in obeying the truth through the Spirit unto unfeigned love of the brethren, see that ye love one another with a pure heart fervently: being born again, not of corruptible seed, but of incorruptible, by the word of God, which liveth and abideth forever."

Not for God to Send Saving Power:

Rom. 1:16. "For I am not ashamed of the gospel of Christ: for it is the power of God unto salvation to every one that believeth."

Not for God to Purify Their Hearts:

Acts 15:9. "And put no difference between us and them, purifying their hearts by faith."

Not for God to Purify Their Soul:

1 Pet. 1:22. "Being born again, not of corruptible seed, but of incorruptible, by the word of God, which liveth and abideth forever."

Not for Freedom From Sin:

Rom. 6:17. "But God be thanked, that ye were the servants of sin, but ye have obeyed from the heart that form of doctrine which was delivered you." Jno. 8:32. "And ye shall

146

know the truth, and the truth shall make you free."

Not for Religion, Because:

Jas. 1:27. "Pure religion and undefiled before God and the Father is this, to visit the fatherless and widows in their afflictions, and to keep himself unspotted from the world."

Not for God to Accept Him:

Acts 10:35. "But in every nation he that feareth him, and worketh righteousness, is accepted with him."

Not for Remission of Sins, Because:

Acts 2:38. Then Peter said unto them, Repent, and be baptized every one of you in the name of Jesus Christ for the remission of sins."

Not to be Made Clean, Because:

Jno. 15:3. "Now ye are clean through the word I have spoken unto you."

Not for Repentance, Because:

Acts 17:30. "And the times of this ignorance God winked at; but now commandeth all men everywhere to repent."

Not for Mercy, For:

Prov. 28:13. "He that covereth his sins shall not prosper; but who so confesseth and forsaketh them shall have mercy."

Not for God to be Willing to Save Him, For:

2 Pet. 3:9. "God is not slack concerning his promise, as some men count slackness; but is longsuffering to us-ward, not willing that any should perish, but that all should come to repentance." Ezk. 18:32. "For I have no pleasure in the death of him that dieth, saith the Lord God: wherefore turn yourself and live ye."

Not for Sanctification:

Jno. 17:17. "Sanctify them through thy truth: thy word is truth."

In Fact, Should He Pray at All?

Jno. 9:31. "Now we know that God heareth not sinners: but if any man be a worshipper of God, and doeth his will, him he heareth." Prov. 1:24-28. "Because I have called, and ye refused; I have stretched out my hand, and no man regarded; but ye have set at naught all my counsel, and would none of my reproof: I also will laugh at your calamity; I will mock when your fear cometh; when your fear cometh as desolation, and your destruction cometh as a whirlwind; when distress and anguish cometh upon you. Then shall they call upon me, but I will not answer." Isa. 59:1-2. "Behold, the Lord's hand is not shortened, that it cannot save; neither is his ear heavy, that it cannot hear: but your iniquities have separated between you and your God, and your sins have hid his face from you, that he will not hear."

A few words about prayer in this connection, contrasting the teaching of the Bible with that of men.

What is the Bible definition of prayer? "My heart's desire and prayer." Rom. 12:1. Prayer is the heart's desire, expressed. "Whatsoever ye do in word or deed, do all in the name of the Lord Jesus, giving thanks to God and the Father by him." Col. 3:17. "Let him ask in faith, nothing wavering. For he that wavereth is like a wave of the sea driven with the wind and tossed. For let not that man think that he shall receive anything of the Lord." Jas. 1:6-7. "And this is the confidence that we have in him, that, if we ask anything according to his will, he heareth
148

us." 1 Jno. 5:14. To sum up: 1. A sincere desire of the heart, expressed. 2. The desire expressed in faith. 3. The desire expressed in the name of Christ. 4. This desire expressed according to his will. If we pray thus, we will have our prayers answered. Asking according to his will is asking as he wills for us to ask. Since I am to ask in his name (by his authority or will), and must ask in faith, and faith comes by hearing the word of God, it is necessary to study the word of God and learn what he wills for me to ask for; and then pray in faith, or my prayer will not be answered.

Prayer must be in faith. Since the man without faith cannot pray in faith, it is strange to me that some teach the sinner to pray for pardon; and at the same time tell them that they are saved the very moment they have faith in Christ. If the sinner is saved the moment he believes in Christ, he cannot pray for salvation, unless he prays before he has faith. James says that the man that asks without faith receives nothing of the Lord. Jas. 1:7. Faith comes by hearing the word of God. It is not possible then to ask in faith till you have been taught the word of God.

Man must come to God to be saved. "He that cometh to God must believe." Heb. 11:6. The sinner must be taught the word of God and believe it before he can come to God. If the sinner must pray, at what point must the praying begin? Not before he is taught the word of God, for that would be praying without faith; and James says such a man will receive nothing of the Lord. Men must be taught before they can pray acceptably. If sinners are saved the moment they believe, I am anxious to know when they are to pray for salvation. If he is saved when he believes, and believes before he prays, then he must be saved before he can pray.

Sinners are in the power of Satan (Acts 26:18), in darkness (Col. 1:13), in the world. You know there is no God, Christ, hope or promise for those in the world. Listen: "Wherefore, remember, that ye being in times past Gentiles in the flesh, . . . that at that time ye were without Christ, being aliens from the commonwealth of Israel, and strangers from the covenants of promise, having no hope, and without God in the world. Eph. 2:11-12. Of his disciples Christ said: "They are not of the world, even as I am not of the world." Jno. 17:16. Again: "Ye are not of the world, but I have chosen you out of the world." Jno. 15:19. Some ask the sinner who is "far off"—from God, Christ, without hope, strangers to the covenants of promise —to come to the altar and pray for God to bless them? Remember: "All the promises of God in him [Christ] are yea, and in him Amen." 2 Cor. 1:20. You must be in Christ to have the promises. It is useless to ask God to bless while you are in the world. In the world you are in the power of Satan, in darkness, and if God blesses you there he blesses in the world. All the blessings are in Christ—not in the world.

Christ is the Mediator of the New Covenant, *not* of the world. Heb. 12:24. Being the Mediator of the New Covenant, and since "no man cometh unto the Father but by me" (Christ) (Jno. 14:6), you see the sinner cannot approach God by prayer, while in the world, unless he can approach God without mediation; and if he can, it will leave Christ out; but

150

Christ says: "No man cometh unto the Father but by me." Christ being Mediator of the New Covenant, only those in the New Covenant—in covenant relationship with God—can approach God through him and be blessed. The sinner must be taught the "word of reconciliation"—hear and learn of God, Christ and salvation; and that he can approach God only through mediation—that Christ is the Mediator; that by lovingly obeying the gospel (word of reconciliation), he comes into covenant relationship with God; that in the covenant, God blesses in Christ. Instead of trying to reach the blessings while in the world, by prayer, men should, by faith, obey God's truth, and by so doing reach the blessings in the New Covenant. Christ is the Mediator of all such.

My brethren are thought selfish because they do not ask the sinners to "come to the altar for prayers." There is certainly a radical difference between what we teach and what many teach along this line. Some are persistently going to God with a petition in behalf of the sinners. We are constantly going to the sinner with a message from God. We desire the salvation of the sinner, but we wish him saved in God's way—the only way. When the sinner cries out (having been taught), "What must we do?" we go to him with God's message—*viz.*, "Repent, and be baptized every one of you in the name of Jesus Christ for the remission of sins." Acts 2:38. Some preachers invite the sinner to the altar to pray. We take no part in such a course; not that we do not want the sinner saved, but we have a message for the sinner from God, and this message we are not welcomed to deliver in such meetings—meetings where the sinner is

151

invited to the altar to pray. They want the sinner saved, but want him saved in their way. We want the sinner saved, but know he can be saved only in God's way. Our love and respect for God and his law is too great to allow us to ask God to set aside his law and save the sinner—sinners can be saved only by obeying the commands of Christ.

"Knowing therefore the terror of the Lord, we persuade men." 2 Cor. 5:11. Contrast this with the action of men who try to "persuade" God. They beg God to bless the sinner, that he may obey. We persuade the sinner to obey God that he may be blessed.

————

PRIESTHOOD CONTRASTED

Old—Tribe of Levi:
Heb. 7:11. "If therefore perfection were by the Levitical priesthood (for under it the people received the law), what further need was there that another priest should rise after the order of Melchisedec, and not be called after the order of Aaron?"

New—Tribe of Juda:
Heb. 7:14. "For it is evident our Lord sprang out of Juda; of which tribe Moses spake nothing concerning priesthood."

Old—Order of Aaron:
Heb. 7:11. "If therefore perfection were by the Levitical priesthood (for under it the people received the law), what further need was there that another priest should rise after the order of Melchisedec, and not be called after the order of Aaron?"

New—Order of Melchisedec:
Heb. 7:17. "Thou art a priest forever after the order of Melchisedec."

Old—Without Oath:

Heb. 7:21. "For those priests were made without an oath."

New—With an Oath:

Heb. 7:21. "For those priests were made without an oath; but this with an oath by him that said unto him, The Lord sware and will not repent, Thou art a priest forever after the order of Melchisedec."

Old—By Law:

Heb. 7:28. "For the law maketh men high priests which have infirmity."

New—By Word of Oath:

Heb. 7:28. "For the law maketh men high priests which have infirmity; but the word of the oath, which was since the law, maketh the Son, who is consecrated for evermore."

Old—Priests Died:

Heb. 7:23. "And they truly were many priests, because they were not suffered to continue by reason of death."

New—Priest Ever Liveth:

Heb. 7:24. "But this man, because he continueth ever, hath an unchangeable priesthood."

Old—Changed:

Heb. 7:12. "For the priesthood being changed, there is made of necessity a change also of the law."

New—Unchangeable:

Heb. 7:24. "But this man, because he continueth ever, hath an unchangeable priesthood."

Old—On Earth:

Heb. 9:7. "But into the second went the high priest alone once every year, not without blood, which he offered for himself, and for the errors of the people."

New—Not on Earth:

Heb. 8:4. "For if he were on earth, he should not be a priest, seeing that there are priests that offer gifts according to the law." Heb. 9:24. "For Christ is not entered into the holy places made with hands, which are the figures of the true; but into heaven itself, now to appear in the presence of God for us."

Priesthood of Christ

From the above you cannot fail to see the difference between the shadow and the substance.

"For the priesthood being changed, there is made of necessity a change also of the law." Heb. 7:12. Christ could not be a priest under the law, for, under the law, the priests had to be of a certain tribe of Israel, and Christ was not of that tribe. While the law was in force, there were priests according to the law. Under the law priests were consecrated "without an oath." Heb. 7:21. Christ was made priest "with an oath." Heb. 7:21. This is proof positive that he was not priest under the law. The Jews knew how to approach God, through the priest, under the law; but if there is a new priesthood, there must be a new law by which to approach God. Jews could not accept Christ as priest and hold to the law; they refused to give up the law, hence rejected Christ. They were like many of this day— did not understand how Christ could be made priest, except by the law. Had Christ claimed to be priest under the law, his claim would have been fraudulent, for he sprang from the tribe of Judah; and according to the law, a man of that tribe could not be priest. Paul tells the Jews that Christ is not priest "after the law of carnal commandments, but after the power of an endless life." Heb. 7:16. "But the word of the oath, which was since the law, maketh the Son, who is consecrated for evermore." Heb. 7:28. The Jews should have understood this, for David spoke of the priesthood of Christ, saying: "The Lord hath sworn, and will not repent, Thou art a priest forever after the order of Melchisedec." Ps. 110:4.

When was Christ inducted into this priestly office? A popular theory is: "John baptized him into his priestly office," or by baptizing him consecrated him a priest. This is incorrect, for under the law, the priests were such by descent—the consecration was not to make them priests; it was God's way to formally set them apart to the priestly office. The Jews knew that under the law the priests were such by descent; they also knew that Christ did not belong to the priestly tribe. Paul says Christ was "without descent."

Again: Christ was made priest "not after the law of a carnal commandment." Heb. 7:16. Remember this!

Some declare: "Christ was consecrated priest by John baptizing him, and in the consecration under the law water was sprinkled on them, therefore the baptism of John was sprinkling." If he was thus made priest, he was made priest "after the law of a carnal commandment;" but Paul says he was not thus made priest. I know all the ordinances of the law were carnal! Proof: "Which stood only in meats and drinks, and divers washings, and carnal ordinances, imposed on them until the time of reformation." Heb. 9:10. This is proof positive that John did not induct Christ into his priestly office. Again:

155

If these sprinklings under the law were baptisms, as Jesus was baptized three and a half years before the law ended, then I have positive proof that John did not baptize him into his priestly office, for Christ was made priest after the law ended. Proof: "But the law maketh men high priests which have infirmity; but the word of the oath, which was since the law, maketh the Son, who is consecrated for evermore." Heb. 7:28. The law could not consecrate one a priest "for evermore," for Paul says, "the law maketh man high priests which have infirmity," and they could not continue, by reason of death. Heb. 7 shows that John, under the law, did not make one a priest "for evermore." I know that John, under the law, did not make Christ a priest, neither did he consecrate him priest; for the law did not continue "for evermore;" hence Christ could not be made priest by a law which ended at his death. As his priesthood is *spiritual*, he could not be made priest by the "carnal commandments" of the law—unless spirituality emanates from carnality—for the law contained only carnal ordinances.

The church of God is God's only spiritual institution in earth; and as the church of God is the "house of God," 1 Tim. 3:15, Paul says "and having a high priest over the house of God," Heb. 10:21, I am certain Christ could not be priest over the house of God—church of God—till God made him "head over all things to the church." God "raised him from the dead, and set him at his own right hand in the heavenly places, far above all principality, and power, . . . and hath put all things under his feet, and gave him to be head over all things to the church, which is his body,

156

the fullness of him that filleth all in all." Eph. 1:20-23. As the church is the "house of God," and we have a "high priest over the house of God," and Jesus was not made head of the church—house of God—till he went to heaven, it surely follows that he was not priest over the house of God till he went to heaven.

There is no law given to man by which one could be consecrated priest after the order of Melchisedec. This is one reason why Christ was not priest while on earth.

"I saw in the night visions, and behold, one like the Son of man came with the clouds of heaven, and came to the Ancient of days, and they brought him near before him. And there was given him dominion, and glory and a kingdom." Dan. 7:13-14. Daniel was speaking of Christ and his ascension to the Father. When he ascended, the Father gave him "dominion, and glory and a kingdom." Again: "Thus speaketh the Lord of hosts, saying, Behold the man whose name is The *Branch*, and he shall grow up out of his place, and he shall build the temple of the Lord: . . . and shall bear the glory, and shall sit and rule upon his throne; and he shall be a priest upon his throne." Zech. 6:12-13. Daniel declared that when Christ went to heaven the Father gave him dominion, glory and a kingdom. From Zechariah we learn that he was to sit and rule upon his throne as priest and king. The facts are: On earth he was not a priest—could not be. Heb. 8:4. He died; the law then ended, and thus ended the Jewish priesthood. This opens the way for another priesthood. He was made priest by "the word of the oath, which was since the law." Heb. 7:28. When he entered heaven, he was given power, placed on the throne, consecrated priest and seven days afterwards made the atonement with "his own blood." Heb. 9:12. The high priest under the law had to stand at the door of the tabernacle seven days before he could make the atonement. Christ went to heaven, was consecrated priest and king, was there seven days, at the end of that time he made the atonement. Since that time no one can approach the Father except through him as the eternal High Priest.

PUNISHMENT.

Punishment:

"Any pain inflicted on a person for a crime or offense."

Everlasting Punishment:

Matt. 25:46. "And these shall go away into everlasting punishment: but the righteous into life eternal." "Everlasting punishment" —"*kolasis.*"

Use of the Word "Punishment"— "Kolasis."

Fear Hath Torment—"Kolasis":

1 Jno. 4:18. "Fear hath torment"—"*kolasin.*"

Punish—Kolasin—Them:

Acts 5:21. "So when they had further threatened them, they let them go, finding nothing how they might punish them."

Reserved to be Punished—"Kolasin":

2 Pet. 2:9. "The Lord knoweth how to deliver the godly out of temptations, and to reserve the unjust unto the day of judgment to be punished"—*kolasin.*

158

Everlasting:

Matt. 25:46. "And these shall go away into everlasting punishment: but the righteous into life eternal." In this passage the words "everlasting" and "eternal" are from the same Greek word.

The Creator Liveth Forever and Ever:

Rev. 10:6. "And sware by him that liveth forever and ever, who created heaven and earth, and the things that therein are."

Tormented Forever and Ever:

Rev. 20:10. "And the devil that deceived them was cast into the lake of fire and brimstone, where the beast and false prophet are, and shall be tormented day and night forever and ever." Does "forever and ever" mean the same in these two passages?

In Heaven it is Always Day:

Rev. 21:25. "And the gates of it shall not be shut at all by day: for there shall be no night there."

In Hell it is Always Night:

Matt. 25:30. "And cast ye the unprofitable servant into outer darkness; there shall be weeping and gnashing of teeth." Rev. 14:11. "And the smoke of their torment ascendeth up forever and ever: and they have no rest day nor night."

Righteous Serve Him Day and Night:

Rev. 7:15. "Therefore are they before the throne of God, and serve him day and night."

Wicked Tormented Day and Night:

Rev. 20:10. "And the devil that deceived them was cast into the lake of fire and brimstone, where the beast and false prophet are, and shall be tormented day and night forever and ever." The saints remain in heaven thru one eternal day—they serve him "day and

159

night." The wicked will be in hell and will be tormented "day and night." If the "day" stops in heaven, or the "night" in hell, then the torment will stop.

Aionios—Everlasting—Eternal.

Everlasting (aionios) God:

Rom. 16:26. "According to the commandment of the everlasting [*aionios*] God."

Eternal (aionios) Spirit:

Heb. 9:14. "How much more shall the blood of Christ, who through the eternal [*aionios*] Spirit offered himself without spot to God?"

Eternal (aionios) Life:

Jno. 3:15. "That whosoever believeth in him should not perish, but have eternal [*aionios*] life."

Eternal (aionios) Life:

Mk. 10:30. "And in the world to come eternal [*aionios*] life."

Everlasting (aionios) Fire:

Matt. 25:41. "Depart from me, ye cursed into everlasting [*aionios*] fire, prepared for the devil and his angels."

Everlasting (aionios) Punishment:

Matt. 25:46. "And these shall go away into everlasting [*aionios*] punishment: but the righteous into life eternal [*aionios*]."

Forever and Ever.

Glory Forever and Forever:

1 Tim. 1:17. "Now unto the King eternal [*aionios*], immortal, invisible, the only wise God, be honor and glory forever and ever."

Glory to God Forever and Ever:

Phil. 4:20. "Now unto God and our Father be glory forever and ever."

Liveth Forever and Ever:

Rev. 10:6. "And sware by him that liveth forever and ever, who created heaven and earth, and the things that therein are."

God Liveth Forever and Forever:

Rev. 15:7. "And one of the four beasts gave unto the seven angels seven golden vials full of the wrath of God, who liveth forever and forever."

Tormented Forever and Forever:

Rev. 20:10. "And the devil that deceived them was cast into the lake of fire and brimstone, where the beast and the false prophet are, and shall be tormented day and night forever and ever."

Who will be "tormented" forever and forever? How long will "forever and ever" be? See use of the word "Torment."

Everlasting Punishment.

Everlasting Punishment:

Matt. 25:46. "And these shall go away into eterlasting [*aionios*] punishment [*kolasin*]: but the righteous into life [*zeon*] eternal [*aionion*]."

Fear Hath Torment:

1 Jno. 4:18. "There is no fear in love; but perfect love casteth out fear; because fear hath torment"—"*kolasin.*"

In each of these passages we have the word "*kolasin.*"

1. "Fear hath torment"—"*kolasin.*"

2. "Wicked will receive everlasting punishment—"*kolasin.*"

What does the word "*kolasin*" mean?

If "eternal punishment" consists in simply dying—dying never to live again—or "ceasing to be," as the annihilationists declare, then every beast of the field will suffer "eternal punishment," for they will "cease to be."

Punishment of the Wicked Will Never End

Cast Into Fire:
Matt. 13:42. "And shall cast them into a furnace of fire: there shall be wailing and gnashing of teeth."

Everlasting Fire:
Matt. 25:41. "Depart from me, ye cursed, into everlasting [*aionios*] fire."

Fire Not Quenched:
Mk. 9:45. "Cast into hell, into the fire that never shall be quenched" [*asbeston*].

1. The wicked will be cast into a "furnace of fire."

2. It is everlasting [*aionion*] fire."

3. Will this fire ever cease? No, it is "unquenched"—asbestos—fire—will never cease.

4. The wicked will receive "everlasting punishment."

5. An "everlasting fire" is fire that never ceases, is unquenchable—asbestos—fire, just so is "everlasting punishment," punishment that never ceases.

6. But punishment is: "Any pain or suffering inflicted on a person for crime or offense."—Webster.

7. Therefore the one punished must exist in a conscious state to be punished.

8. "And they shall be tormented day and night forever and ever." Rev. 20:10.

Use of the Word "Torment"—"Basanizo."

My Son is Tormented:

Matt. 8:6. "Lord, my son is at home sick with the palsy, grievously tormented."

Tormented for Five Months:

Rev. 9:5. "And to them it was given that they should not kill them, but that they should be tormented [*basunisthosi*] five months: and their torment [*basanismos*] was as the torment [*basanismos*] of a scorpion, when he striketh a man." "Tormented" for five months, like the "torment" of a serpent bite. Were they unconscious while thus tormented? If they must be conscious to be "tormented" for five months, can they be "tormented" forever, if they are not conscious forever?

Lot "Vexed"—Tormented:

2 Pet. 2:7-8. "And delivered just Lot, vexed with the filthy conversation of the wicked: (for that righteous man dwelling among them, in seeing and hearing, vexed [*ebasanizen*—tormented] his righteous soul from day to day . . .)" Could he have "vexed"—tormented—his soul from day to day, if he had been unconsious?

Tormented Forever and Ever:

Rev. 20:10. "And the devil that deceived them was cast into the lake of fire and brimstone, where the beast and false prophet are, and shall be tormented [*basanisthesontai*] day and night forever and ever." How long will this "torment" be? Can that which does not exist be "tormented"? Can that which is unconsious be "tormented"?

Punishment—Destruction.

Everlasting Destruction:

2 Thess. 1:9. "Who shall be punished with everlasting destruction from the presence of the Lord, and the glory of his power."

Tribulation and Anguish:

Rom. 2:8-9. "But unto them that are contentious, and do not obey the truth, but obey unrighteousness, indignation and wrath, tribulation and anguish, upon every soul of man that doeth evil; the Jew first and also the Gentile."

1. In the first passage it is stated that the wicked will be punished with "everlasting destruction."

2. In the second passage it is stated that the punishment will be "tribulation and anguish."

3. Therefore, "destruction" when used in reference to punishment of the wicked means "tribulation and anguish."

4. How long will they suffer "tribulation and anguish"? Let Paul answer: "Punished with everlasting destruction," or substituting his own meaning of the term, it is "everlasting tribulation and anguish."

5. Those who believe in annihilation admit that "everlasting" in the first passage is without limitation—that it is a destruction that will never cease.

6. Therefore the "tribulation and anguish" of the wicked will never cease.

7. But "tribulation and anguish" necessitates consciousness.

Punishment—Destroy
(Apolesai), Lost.

Destroy Body and Soul in Hell:

Matt. 10:28. "And fear not them which kill the body, but are not able to kill the soul: but rather fear him which is able to destroy [*apolesai*] both soul and body in hell." Does the word "destroy" (*apolesai*) mean annihilate?

Lose a Sheep:

Lk. 15:4. "What man of you having an hundred sheep, if he lose [*apolesai*] one of them, doth not leave the ninety and nine in the wilderness and go after that which is lost [*apololos*], until he find it?"

Found the "Lost" Sheep:

Lk. 15:5-6. "And when he hath found it, he layeth it on his shoulders, rejoicing. And when he cometh home, he calleth together his friends and neighbors, saying unto them, Rejoice with me; I have found my sheep which was lost [*apololos*]."

Lose Money:

Lk. 15:8-9. "What woman having ten pieces of silver, if she lose [*apolese*] one piece, doth not light a candle, and sweep the house, and seek diligently till she find it. And when she hath found it, she calleth her friends and her neighbors together, saying, Rejoice with me; for I have found the piece which was lost [*apolesa*]." Though the sheep was *apolesas*, it was found—it had not been annihilated. The piece of silver was *apolese*, but it was not annihilated. Then why do some people insist that the soul through *apolesai* in hell, means that it will be annihilated—that it will cease to exist?

Blotted Out—Destroy.

Wicked Blotted Out:

Gen. 6:7. "And the Lord said, I will destroy man whom I have created from the face of the earth."

Blot Out of Book:

Ex. 32:3. "Whosoever hath sinned against me, him will I blot out of my book."

Blot Out Iniquities:

Ps. 51:9. "Blot out all mine iniquities."

Blot Out Ordinances:

Col. 2:14. "Blotting out the handwriting of ordinances that was against us."

In these passages the words "destroy" and "blot out" are from the Hebrew word "*Machah.*" This word does not imply "annihilation;" for when "sins" are "blotted out" they are not "annihilated." A fact, a deed, is not susceptible of "annihilation." It may be forgiven, perchance forgotten, but not undone. When the ordinances of the law were "blotted out" they did not cease to exist; they merely became inoperative.

Destroyed.

Wicked Destroyed:

Ps. 5:6. "Thou shalt destroy them that speak leasing."

Wicked Will Be Destroyed:

Ps. 145:20. "The Lord preserveth all them that love him: but all the wicked will be destroyed."

Sinners Destroyed:

Isa. 13:9. "Behold, the day of the Lord cometh, cruel both with wrath and fierce anger, to lay the land desolate: and he shall destroy the sinners thereof out of it."

Destroyed, Yet Alive:

Job 19:10. "He hath destroyed me on every side, and I am gone: and mine hope hath he removed like a tree."

Destroyed, Yet Existing:

Hos. 4:6. "My people are destroyed for lack of knowledge."

Help for Those Destroyed:

Hos. 13:9. "O Israel, thou hast destroyed thyself; but in me is thine help." If the word "destroy" in these passages means extinction, or the termination of conscious existence, we have, in the last citation, a people, though annihilated, in a hopeful condition. A strange kind of annihilation.

Destruction—Destruction.

Jer. 4:20. "Destruction upon destruction is cried." If "destruction" means "annihilation," how do you account for this language—does it mean "annihilate" twice?

Double Destruction:

Jer. 17:18. "Let them be confounded that persecute me. But let me not be confounded: let them be dismayed, but let not me be dismayed: bring upon them the day of evil, and destroy them double with destruction." "Annihilate" them twice, eh?

Perish.

The Wicked Perish:

Ps. 37:20. "But the wicked shall perish."

God's Enemies Perish:

Jud. 5:31. "So let all thine enemies perish, O Lord."

Liars Perish:

Prov. 19:9. "He that speaketh lies shall perish."

Just Man Perishes:

Eccl. 7:15. "All things have I seen in the days of my vanity: there is a just man that perished in his righteousness."

The Righteous Perished:

Isa. 57:1. "The righteous perisheth, and no man layeth it to heart."

The Good Man Perisheth:

Mic. 7:2. "The good man is perished out of the earth."

In all these verses the same Hebrew term, "*Abadh,*" is used. If the first three passages mean that the wicked will be "annihilated," is it clear, and with equal force must follow, the last three passages teach that the righteous will be "annihilated." Such is the conclusion literalism drives one to.

Cut Off.

Evil Doers "Cut Off":

Ps. 37:9. "For evil doers shall be cut off."

Wicked Are "Cut Off":

Ps. 37:34. "When the wicked are cut off."

The Messiah "Cut Off":

Dan. 9:36. "And after threescore and two weeks shall Messiah be cut off." In these three passages the word "*Karath*" is rendered "cut off." If the first two teach the "annihilation" of the wicked, then the last passage teaches the Messiah was "annihilated."

Was Not.

Wicked "Was Not":

Ps. 37:35-36. "I have seen the wicked in great power, and spreading himself like a green bay tree. Yet he passed away, and, lo, he was not."

Enoch "Was Not":

Gen. 5:24. "And Enoch walked with God: and was not; for God took him." The Hebrew word for "was not" is exactly the same in each of these passages. If the first teaches the "annihilation" of the wicked, the second certainly teaches the "annihilation" of Enoch; but he did not see death. Heb. 11:5.

Consume and Devour.

The Jews Consumed:

Jer. 5:3. "O Lord, are not thine eyes upon the truth? thou hast stricken them, but they are not grieved; thou hast consumed them, but they have refused to receive correction: they have made their faces harder than a rock; they have refused to return."

Jacob Consumed:

Jer. 10:25. "Pour out thy fury upon the heathen that know thee not, and upon the families that call not on thy name: for they have eaten up Jacob and devoured him, and consumed him."

Zeal Consumes Me:

Ps. 119:139. "My zeal hath consumed me."

Consumed by Anger:

Ps. 90:7. "For we are consumed by thine anger."

What reasonable man can entertain that "consume" or "devour" means to annihilate?

Wicked Devoured:

Rev. 20:9. "And fire came down from God out of heaven, and devoured them."

Devour Each Other:

Gal. 5:15. "But if ye bite and devour one another, take heed that ye be not consumed one of another."

Consumed.

Sinners Consumed:

Ps. 104:35. "Let the sinners be consumed out of the earth."

Forsake the Lord—Consumed:

Isa. 1:28. "And the destruction of the transgressors and of the sinners shall be together, and they that forsake the Lord shall be consumed."

Scorners Consumed:

Isa. 29:20. "For the terrible one is brought to naught, and the scorner is consumed."

Hailstones Consume a Wall:

Ezk. 13:12-13. "Lo, when the wall is fallen, shall it not be said unto you, Where is the daubing wherewith ye have daubed it? Therefore thus saith the Lord God; I will even rend it with a stormy wind in my fury; there shall be an overflowing shower in mine anger, and great hailstones in my fury to consume it."

Mountains Consumed:

Ezk. 35:12. "And thou shalt know that I am the Lord, and that I have heard all thy blasphemies which thou hast spoken against the mountains of Israel, saying, They are laid desolate, they are given us to consume."

Of course a "wall" consumed by "hailstones" and "mountains" consumed by "men" does not mean that they ceased to exist—annihilated.

Come To An End.

Wicked Have An End:

Num. 24:20. "Amalek was the first of the nations; but his latter end shall be that he perish forever."

Sinners Have An End:

Phil. 3:19. "Whose end is destruction."

Righteous Have An End:

Num. 23:10. "Let me die the death of the righteous, and let my last end be like his."

End of Perfect Man:

Ps. 37:37. "Mark the perfect man, and behold the upright: for the end of that man is peace."

If the "end" of the wicked will be "annihilation," what will the end of the righteous be?

Second Death.

Once to Die:

Heb. 9:27. "It is appointed unto men once to die, but after this the judgment." It has never been appointed unto men to die twice—but once to die. This does not mean that all men *must* die even *once,* for those who are changed when the Lord comes will not die. It but means that men may die one time. Those who insist that men may die twice dispute the word of Paul.

Second Death:

Rev. 2:11. "He that overcometh shall not be hurt of the second death."

What is Second Death?

Rev. 20:14. "And death and hell were cast into the lake of fire. This is the second death."

What is Second Death?

Rev. 21:8. "But the fearful, and unbelieving, and the abominable, and murderers, and idolators, and all liars, shall have their part in the lake which burneth with fire and brimstone: which is the second death." Will you please observe that it is not intimated that anyone dies in that lake? "Death and hell were cast into the lake of fire." Rev. 20:14. Who would think of saying that "death" died, or that "hell" died in the lake? Indeed, the place—the "lake of fire and brimstone"— is the second death. The place is called the "second death" and it is not one time intimated that anyone dies in that place.

Cast **Alive** *Into the Lake:*

Rev. 19:20. "And the beast was taken, and with him the false prophet that wrought miracles before him, with which he deceived them that had received the mark of the beast, and them that worshiped his image. These both were cast *alive* into a lake of fire burning with brimstone." There is not an intimation that those who are cast into the lake will die again, but that the lake is the second death, and that in it they are to be punished.

It is appointed unto man once to die. The dead are raised, and the wicked are cast *alive* into the lake, and this lake is the second death. If the wicked die again, then it is appointed unto them to die *twice*, but inspiration declares that it is appointed unto man to die *once*.

Annihilation.
Objections—Questions.

1. It makes no distinction between the state of the sinner before and after the resur-

172

rection. Per the doctrine of those who teach "annihilation" the wicked are raised from a state of "non-existence," to consign them to the same state again. If they are right, why raise the sinner from a state of non-existence, to consign them to the same state again?

2. The doctrine makes no distinction in the degrees of punishment. Matt. 23:14; Lk. 12:47-48.

3. The doctrine makes death the extreme penalty of the law, in opposition to the scripture which speaks of a "much sorer punishment" than death for those who do "despite to the spirit of grace." Heb. 10:28. "Sorer" or "worse." Matt. 9:16; 12:45; 27:64; Mk. 5:26; Jno. 5:14; 2 Pet. 2:20; 1 Tim. 5:8.

4. It makes the punishment—state of the wicked—consist of simply non-existence, in direct opposition to the scriptures which represent it as conscious suffering. Lk. 13:28-38; Rom. 2:8-9.

5. The doctrine of the annihilation of the wicked makes the suffering of the wicked terminate at death, or, at most at the judgment, in opposition to the scripture which declares it will be "everlasting punishment." Matt. 25:46.

6. If death is the punishment, the simple punishment, the whole of the punishment of the wicked, then since the righteous die, they will suffer as much as the wicked.

7. The annihilation of the wicked stamps as a deception the horrors of the punishment of the wicked as well as the happiness of the righteous.

8. The doctrine of annihilation is a prime doctrine of infidelity.

173

Questions.

1. If burning up, literally, is the eternal punishment of the wicked, can't man inflict it? If not, why?

2. Can man suffer "eternal punishment" twice?

3. If the punishment of the wicked will simply be "burning them up," did not some of the martyrs—those burned at the stake—suffer as much as the wicked will?

4. Can the unconscious be tormented?

5. Will the world be burned up? 2 Pet. 3:10. Will it not exist after being burned?

6. If the wicked cease to exist, will not the punishment cease?

7. Can man who has "never been" be punished?

8. If the wicked, at death, become as "though they had never been," how can they be punished?

9. Is punishment that ceases "everlasting punishment"? If yes, may not "everlasting life" cease, and still be "everlasting life"?

I am certain that the above is a complete refutation of the theory that annihilation is the punishment of God for the wicked. Punishment is "pain inflicted on a person for a crime," and those who hold to annihilation know no punishment for sin, except a corporal punishment. With them the only pain inflicted for a long life in sin is but a few minutes of bodily suffering and all is ended. They insist that the sinner loses his identity —becomes as though he had never been. If such be true, there is no such thing as "eternal punishment." In fact, the duration of punishment is so short that it is not worthy the name of "time punishment," much less eternal. In order to reach the conclusion that all punishment is corporal, or bodily punishment, it must be established that all the consciousness man has, or can have, is consciousness of the organic matter which constitutes the body of each individual. With them there can be no such things as mental suffering, unless mind is matter. If mind is matter, it is a part of our corporal organism, and as the body is changed in the resurrection, of course the mind will be changed. As we are changed from natural to spiritual, it follows that no one can be spiritual-minded till after the resurrection. If this be true, then man can have only natural or fleshly mind till after the resurrection. To admit that mind is not matter, is to admit that it cannot be burned as matter. You cannot burn the intelligence of man by burning the body. Paul "rejoiced in afflictions." He suffered much physically, but had great mental joy. I am curious to know how there can be mental joy, where there is pain of the body, if the mind is part of the body. If one can have mental joy, where there is bodily pain, and they can, can't one have great mental pain where there is bodily suffering? If the burning of the body is the final punishment for sin, is it not a fact that a poor dog that is burned, suffers as much as the vilest sinner?

God cannot punish a lie! But, if man be purely physical, when he lies it is naught more than a physical act. This being true, a lie partakes of the nature of organic matter— is a part of the same. Remember, I am reasoning from the assumption that man is all matter. Character, good, bad or indifferent, is not matter. None but intelligent beings (mankind) have character. Character is not the act of the being, but a principle of right or wrong manifested by said acts. Character being a principle that is the result of intelligent acts, acts of intelligent beings, they act the principle of right that is in the law of right, or the principle of wrong that is in the law of wrong. Character is formed in the intelligence of the being, and manifested in the intelligence controlling our acts. You cannot punish character, neither can you destroy character. Character is a principle, and you cannot destroy a principle, neither can you punish it. The person can be punished for perpetuating a character of evil, or rewarded for a character of righteousness. If the righteous character is eternal, why not the opposite, seeing both are principles?

The Annihilationist declares the mind (spirit) is no part of the man. Paul says the spirit of man knows the things of man. 1 Cor. 2:11. James declares, "the body without the spirit is dead." If the spirit is no part of the man, of course the spirit cannot be punished. As the man without the spirit is dead, and you cannot punish a dead thing, then the man, the entire man of the Annihilationist, which is the body only, can be burned up, but not punished; for the body, after the spirit has left it, has eyes, but sees not, ears but hears not, tongue but speaks not—it is dead, inanimate, inert, unconscious—it cannot be punished.

The principles of good and evil are eternal. Justice demands as a reward for good, eternal happiness; for the evil, eternal misery. Nothing short of this will satisfy divine justice.

REPENTANCE.

Repent or Perish:

Lk. 13:3. "Except ye repent, ye shall all likewise perish."

Command to Repent:

Acts 17:30. "And the times of this ignorance God winked at; but now commandeth all men everywhere to repent."

Repent Unto Life:

Acts 11:18. "Then hath God also to the Gentiles granted repentance unto life."

Heaven is Interested:

Lk. 15:7. "I say unto you, that likewise joy shall be in heaven over one sinner that repenteth, more than over ninety and nine just persons, which need no repentance."

Warning From Hell to Repent:

Lk. 16:27-30. "Then he said, I pray thee therefore, father, that thou wouldest send him to my father's house: for I have five brothers; that he may testify unto them, lest they also come to this place of torment. Abraham said unto him, They have Moses and the prophets; let them hear them. And he said, Nay, father Abraham: but if one went unto them from the dead, they will repent."

What Is Repentance?

Not Godly Sorrow:

2 Cor. 7:10. "For godly sorrow worketh repentance."

Not Reformation:

Matt. 3:8. "Bring forth therefore fruits worthy of repentance."

It is Change of Will:

Matt. 21:28-29. "But what think ye? A certain man had two sons; and he came to the first, and said, Son, go work today in my vineyard. He answered and said, I will not: but afterwards he repented, and went."

Motives To Repentance.

Fear of Judgment:
Acts 17:30-31. "And the times of this ignorance God winked at; but now commandeth all men everywhere to repent: because he hath appointed a day, in the which he will judge the world in righteousness."

Goodness of God:
Rom. 2:4. "The goodness of God leadeth thee to repentance."

Repentance Before Faith.

The above scriptures teach the necessity of repentance, and what it is.

Sorrow is not repentance, yet one cannot repent who does not sorrow on account of sin. Repentance is a change of will and with it is a deep conviction of sorrow, which brings about a reformation of life, or turning from sin—evil—and doing right.

You find a thief, when caught, very sorry; but when freed, steals again. He was not sorry that he had stolen, but sorry that he was caught. A drunkard claims at times that he is sorry he got drunk. He gets drunk time and time again. The truth is, he is not sorry he got drunk, but sorry the "drunk" made him sick. Had there been the deep conviction of remorse—shame—that caused him to say: "I'm sorry I have disgraced myself, I'll quit," and then quit, that would have been repentance. We are agreed that repentance in a Bible sense brings about a reformation of life—a turning from wrong to the right.

To hear a man preach: "Repentance precedes faith," seems strange to one who understands how to rightly divide the word of God. The Jews were taught by John the Baptist, the twelve and the seventy, under the first commission, "To repent and believe the gospel." To "repent," for the kingdom of heaven is at hand. To repent and believe on him that shall come. Remember, these Jews were God's children, under the first covenant, and John was sent to them, preaching repentance. They had left the law, and the worship under the law. They were believers in God, but had ceased to worship him as the law directed. Jesus said to them: "Ye hypocrites, well did Esaias prophesy of you, saying, This people draweth nigh unto me with their mouth, and honoreth me with their lips; but their heart is far from me. But in vain do they worship me, teaching for doctrines the commandments of men." Matt. 15:7-9. You see why they were commanded to repent. To take these scriptures and apply them to alien sinners is a perversion of God's word. When they truly repented, they turned from the doctrines and commandments of men to God's law: As the law was "our schoolmaster to bring us to Christ." Gal. 3:24. They had left the means by which they could reach Christ. Hence, they were told to repent—turn to the law, do God's commandments, and believe the glad tidings of the near approach of the reign of the Messiah. They had the law of God, were subjects of that law, but had turned from it. God commanded them to repent—it was necessary for them to turn to the law. Christ and his kingdom had not come, but they were told to believe the glad tidings of the near

179

approach of both the Messiah and the kingdom. The Jews could do that, for they had violated the law, and the gospel of the kingdom was preached to them—in fact, it was not sent to others; the apostles were forbidden to preach to the Gentiles (Matt. 10:5) at that time.

But is one taught now to repent and believe the glad tidings of the near approaching kingdom of Christ? No. Why? Because Christ and his kingdom have come. Another reason why I say "no" is: If a man repents before he believes the gospel, repentance could not be a part of the gospel. Why? If you repent before you believe the gospel, you repent before you have heard the gospel; for faith comes by hearing the word of God. Rom. 10:17. Since you must hear the gospel before you can believe it, if you repent before you have faith, you repent before you have heard the gospel, and repentance cannot be part of the gospel. But if people now must "repent and believe the gospel," the apostles preached it this way: "You repent and believe the gospel of Christ, but you cannot call on the Lord till you believe, and you cannot believe till you hear. Repent of your sins, and we will preach the gospel to you, when you hear you can believe, but you can't believe till you repent, and it would be foolishness to preach to you that you might believe, knowing you cannot believe till you repent. True, the Lord said for you to believe on him through our words, and true that we preach nothing but the gospel, but you must repent ere you can believe a word we preach." If repentance precedes faith, it must stand as the above.

The apostles preached "repentance and remission of sins" in the name (by the authority) of Christ. But the apostles preached nothing but the gospel. Christ said for all to believe on him through their words. "He that believeth not is condemned already because he hath not believed in the name [authority] of the only begotten Son of God." Jno. 3:18. The man is under condemnation till he believes. How is he to believe? "Believe on me through their words." Jno. 17:20. If man must repent before he believes, then repentance is no part of the gospel, for man must believe the gospel. Man does not believe in repentance, if he repents before he believes. Repentance is no part of faith, if it precedes faith. If it is no part of faith, it is not necessary to salvation, for man is saved by faith. "He that cometh to God must believe" before he can come to God. If he repents before he believes, then repentance cannot be coming to God, nor is it any part of that which is necessary for me to do to come to God.

Those who preach repentance before faith preach under the wrong commission.

THE SABBATH.

The Sabbath was first mentioned in Ex. 16.

The Sabbath is the seventh, not the first day.

Ex. 20:10. "But the seventh day is the Sabbath of the Lord."

When Given:

Neh. 9:13-14. "Thou camest down also upon Mount Sinai, and spakest with them from heaven, and gavest them right judgments, and true laws, good statutes and commandments: and madest known unto them thy holy sabbath, and commandedst them precepts, statutes, and laws, by the hand of Moses thy servant."

Given Not to Fathers:

Deut. 5:1-14. "And Moses called all Israel, and said unto them, Hear, O Israel, the statutes and judgments which I speak in your ears this day, and do them. The Lord God made a covenant with us in Horeb. The Lord made not this convenant with our fathers, but with us, even us, who are all of us here alive this day. . . . I am the Lord thy God, which brought thee out of the land of Egypt, from the house of bondage. Thou shalt have none other gods before me. . . . Keep the sabbath day to sanctify it, as the Lord hath commanded thee. . . . But the seventh day is the sabbath of the Lord thy God: in it thou shalt not do any work."

Was a Sign Between God and Israel:

Ex. 31:17. "It is a sign between me and the children of Israel forever."

Why Given:

Deut. 5:15. "And remember that thou wast a servant in the land of Egypt, and that the Lord thy God brought thee out thence through a mighty hand and by a stretched-out arm: therefore the Lord thy God commanded thee to keep the sabbath-day." Were you—Gentiles—servants in the land of Egypt?

The Ten Commandments Were Called the Covenant:

Ex. 34:28. "And he was there with the Lord forty days and forty nights; he did neither eat bread nor drink water. And he wrote upon the tables the words of the covenant, the ten commandments."

182

His Covenant, The Ten Commandments:

Deut. 4:13. "And he declared unto you his covenant, which he commanded you to perform, even ten commandments; and he wrote them upon two tables of stone."

Tables of Covenant—Two Tables of Stone:

Deut. 9:9-11. "When I was gone up into the mount, to receive the tables of stone, even the tables of the covenant which the Lord made with you, then I abode in the mount forty days and forty nights, I neither did eat bread, nor drink water: and the Lord delivered unto me two tables of stone written with the finger of God; and on them was written according to all the words which the Lord spake with you in the mount, out of the midst of the fire, in the day of the assembly. And it came to pass at the end of forty days and forty nights, that the Lord gave me the two tables of stone, even the tables of the covenant."

Made This Covenant When Brought Out of Egypt:

1 Kings 8:9-21. "There was nothing in the ark save the two tables of stone, which Moses put there at Horeb, when the Lord made a covenant with the children of Israel, when they came out of the land of Egypt. . . . And I have set there a place for the ark, wherein is the covenant of the Lord, which he made with our fathers, when he brought them out of the land of Egypt."

Was the Covenant That Was Made When They Came From Egypt Taken Away?

New Covenant Promised:

Jer. 31:31-34. "Behold, the days come, saith the Lord, that I will make a new covenant with the house of Israel, and with the house of Judah: not according to the covenant that I made with their fathers, in the day that I took them by the hand to bring them out of the land of Egypt; which my covenant they brake, although I was an husband unto them, saith the Lord: But this shall be the covenant that I will make with the house of Israel; After those days, saith the Lord, I will put my law in their inward parts, and write it in their hearts; and will be their God and they shall be my people."

New Covenant Has Been Made:

Heb. 8:6-13. "But now hath he obtained a more excellent ministry, by how much also he is the mediator of a better covenant, which was established upon better promises. For if that first covenant had been faultless, then should no place have been sought for the second. For finding fault with them, he said, Behold, the days come, saith the Lord, when I will make a new covenant with the house of Israel and with the house of Judah. Not according to the covenant that I made with their fathers, in the day when I took them by the hand to lead them out of the land of Egypt: because they continued not in my covenant, and I regarded them not, saith the Lord. . . . In that he saith, a new covenant, he hath made the first old."

Ministers of New Covenant:

2 Cor. 3:6-14. "Who also hath made us able ministers of the new testament; not of the letter, but of the spirit: for the letter killeth, but the spirit giveth life. But if the ministration of death, written *and* engraven in stones, was glorious, so that the children of Israel could not steadfastly behold the face of Moses for the glory of his countenance;

184

which *glory* was to be done away: how shall not the ministration of the spirit be rather glorious? For if the ministration of condemnation *be* glory, much more doth the ministration of righteousness exceed in glory. For even that which was made glorious had no glory in this respect, by reason of the glory that excelleth. For if that which is done away *was* glorious, much more that which remaineth *is* glorious. Seeing then that we have such hope, we use great plainness of speech: and not as Moses, *which* put a veil over his face, that the children of Israel could not steadfastly look to the end of that which is abolished: But their minds were blinded: for until this day remaineth the same veil untaken away in the reading of the old testament; which *veil* is done away in Christ.''

Handwriting of Ordinances Taken Away:

Col. 2:14. "Blotting out the handwriting of ordinances that was against us, which was contrary to us, and took it out of the way, nailing it to his cross.''

The Ten Commandments are the only handwriting God ever had, so far as we know. The Ten Commandments were written with the finger of God. Ex. 31:18.

Advents Say the "Law of Moses" Has Been Taken.

Circumcised on Sabbath:

Jno. 7:22-23. "Moses therefore gave unto you circumcision (not because it is of Moses, but of the fathers); and ye on the sabbath-day circumcise a man. If a man on the sabbath-day receive circumcision, that the law of Moses should not be broken, are ye angry at me, because I have made a man every whit whole on the sabbath day?''

185

Law of Moses Includes the Ten Commandments.

Moses Gave the Law:

Jno. 7:19. "Did not Moses give you the law, and *yet* none of you keepeth the law? Why go ye about to kill me?" This is the Sixth Commandment.

Mk. 7:10. "For Moses said, Honor thy father and thy mother; and, Whoso curseth father or mother, let him die the death." This is the Fifth Commandment.

Book of the Law of Moses.

The following citations refer to the "Book of the Law of Moses": 2 Kings 14:6; 2 Chr. 35:12; Ezk. 6:18; Jno. 8:31; 1 Cor. 14:34. But these refer respectively to: Deut. 24:16; Lev. 3:3; Num. 3:6; Ex. 20:25; Gen. 3:16. Thus Genesis, Exodus, Leviticus, Numbers, and Deuteronomy are called the "Book of the Law of Moses." Advents know nothing about the Ten Commandments, save as they learn them from the Book of the Law of Moses. See Neh. 8:1-8, 18.

Greatest Commandment:

Matt. 22:36-40. "Master, which is the greatest commandment in the law? Jesus said unto him, Thou shalt love the Lord thy God with all thy heart, and with all thy soul, and with all thy mind. This is the first and greatest commandment. And the second is like unto it, Thou shalt love thy neighbor as thyself. On these two commandments hang all the law and prophets." Jesus here makes reference to Deut. 6:5. Advents think the Law of God and the Law of Moses are different; that the Law of Moses has been "done away." The above commandments are not in what Advents call the "law of God," but what they call the "law of Moses." Thus by their foolishness they make the "greatest commandments" in the "law of Moses" which has been done away.

Sheep Killing Each Sabbath:

Num. 28:9-10. "And on the Sabbath day two lambs of the first year without spot, and two tenth-deals of flour for a meat offering, mingled with oil, and the drink offering thereof: This is the burnt-offering of every sabbath." If there is a sabbath now, it is one of "every sabbath," and the above mentioned offering belongs to it.

A Gentile, as such, was never commanded to keep the Sabbath.

The scriptures above teach who the Sabbath was given to, and why it was given. It was binding on no one save Israel of old. Paul said the Gentiles had not the law. Rom. 2:14. Again: "We know that what things soever the law saith, it saith to them who are under the law." Rom. 3:19. It stands thus: The Jews had the law, the law said for them to keep the Sabbath. The law said things to only those who were under the law. The Gentiles did not have the law. Therefore the law said nowhere for the Gentiles to keep the Sabbath.

"For the promise, that he should be heir of the world, was not of Abraham, or his seed, through the law, but through the righteousness of faith. For if they which are of the law be heirs, faith is made void, and the promise made of none effect." Rom. 4:13-14. Paul contrasts the "righteousness of faith" with "the law." He says: "If they which are of the law be heirs, faith is void, and the promise made of none effect." Advents say we must keep the "law." God says the promise is not by the law. Advents say it is. I am sure God knows.

Righteousness is the commandment of God. Ps. 119:172. "But the righteousness of God without the law is manifested"—(or made manifest). Rom. 3:21. Since "righteousness" of God is "commandments of God" and "righteousness of God" is manifest without the law, it follows that there are commands of God without "the law." What "righteousness" (commands) is this? "Even the righteousness of God which is by faith of Jesus Christ." Rom. 3:22. (The Greek says "the faith of Jesus Christ.") Commandments is righteousness. "The faith" is the gospel of Christ. Then the "righteousness of God which is by the faith of Jesus" is the commands of God in the gospel of Christ. Then the promise is not by keeping the law, but by doing the commands of the gospel. The righteousness of God is without the deeds of the law; the righteousness of God is revealed in the gospel. Rom. 1:17. Where is boasting then? It is excluded. By what law? of works? Nay: but by the law of faith." Rom. 3:27. "Behold, thou art called a Jew, and restest in the law, and makest thy boast of God." Rom. 2:17. The Advent, like the Jew, is boasting in the law. Paul says such boasting is excluded, "by the law of faith."

"Before faith came, we were kept under the law, shut up under the faith which should afterwards be revealed." Gal. 3:23. Since "the faith" is the gospel, then the gospel was revealed since the law. The righteousness of God is commandments of God, but the righteousness of God is revealed in the gospel.

Rom. 1:17. Man is justified by the law of faith; not by the law—law of Moses. "By the deeds of the law shall no flesh be justified in his sight." Rom. 3:20. "But that no man is justified by the law in the sight of God is evident: for, The just shall live by faith [the faith]. And the law is not of faith." Gal. 3:11-12. "Knowing that a man is not justified by the works of the law, but by the faith of Jesus Christ, even we have believed in Jesus Christ, that we might be justified by the faith of Christ, and not by the works of the law: for by the works of the law shall no flesh be justified." Gal. 2:16.

There is not a command in "the faith"—the gospel—for any man to keep the sabbath.

IS SALVATION CONDITIONAL?

Believe—Thou Shalt Be Saved:

Acts 16:31. "Believe on the Lord Jesus Christ, and thou shalt be saved and thy house."

Obey—Eternal Salvation:

Heb. 5:9. "He became the author of eternal salvation unto all them that obey him."

Believing to Saving of Soul:

Heb. 10:39. "But we are not of them who draw back unto perdition; but of them that believe to the saving of the soul."

Salvation Nearer:

Rom. 13:11. "Now is our salvation nearer than when we believed."

Save Them That Believe:

1 Cor. 1:21. "It pleased God by the foolishness of preaching to save them that believe."

Believe Not—Die in Sins:

Jno. 8:24. "I said therefore unto you, that ye shall die in your sins; for if you believe not that I am he, ye shall die in your sins."

Repent or Perish:

Lk. 13:3. "Except ye repent, ye shall all likewise perish."

Must We Do Anything To Be Saved?

Do Will—Enter Kingdom:

Matt. 7:21-24. "Not every one that saith unto me, Lord, Lord, shall enter into the kingdom of heaven; but he that doeth the will of my Father which is in heaven."

What Must I Do?

Matt. 19:16. "And, behold, one came and said unto him, Good Master, what good thing shall I do, that I may have eternal life?"

What Shall We Do:

Acts 2:37. "Now when they heard this, they were pricked in their heart, and said unto Peter and the rest of the apostles, Men and brethren, what shall we do?"

Must Do:

Acts 9:6. "And he trembling and astonished said, Lord, what wilt thou have me to do? And the Lord said unto him, Arise, and go into the city, and it shall be told thee what thou must do."

What Must I Do:

Acts 16:30. "Sirs, what must I do to be saved?"

Done Good—Life:

Jno. 5:28, 29. "The hour is coming, in the which all that are in the graves shall hear his voice, and shall come forth; they that have done good, unto the resurrection of life; and they that have done evil, unto the resurrection of damnation.''

Obey Him—Life:

Heb. 5:8-9. "Though he were a Son, yet learned he obedience by the things which he suffered; and being made perfect, he became the author of eternal salvation unto all them that obey him.''

Obey Not Gospel—Vengeance:

2 Thess. 1:7-8. "The Lord Jesus shall be revealed from heaven with his mighty angels, in flaming fire taking vengeance on them that know not God, and that obey not the gospel of our Lord Jesus Christ.''

Do Commandments—Enter:

Rev. 22:14. "Blessed are they that do his commandments, that they may have right to the tree of life, and may enter in through the gates into the city.''

Is salvation conditional? is one of the most important subjects in the Bible. Do we have to do anything to be saved? Some people teach that man has nothing to do—in fact, can do nothing that will in any way result in his salvation or bring his salvation about. They teach that only God's children can obey his law. They say there are two classes—*viz.,* God's children, the elect; and the non-elect. Elect means chosen, and they say the elect were chosen as God's children to be saved before the foundation of the world, chosen to be saved both in time and eternity. If this be true, they will not be saved because of anything they say or do; for their salvation was secured before they had an existence. The non-elect were such before they had a being, and for that reason are not condemned because of anything they have done. If this

191

theory be true, sinners are not under condemnation for anything they do; they were condemned before they sinned. Indeed, they sinned because they were non-elect. Hence, no one is condemned for sinning, nor is anyone saved from sin; they are saved before they existed, saved before they could sin. While this is the legitimate conclusion from their premise, they declare that elect and non-elect are alike depraved at birth; that those among the depraved who are God's elect, he will reveal to them by a dream, vision or impression, that they were saved before the foundation of the world. Those who do not receive such impression are of the non-elect. This leaves them in suspense till they are made to know that they are among the elect. Am I right in stating their position? Hear Wesley in his work, "Original Sin," page 340: "We are by nature the children of wrath; we are worthy of and liable to the wrath of God, and that by nature; therefore we are, doubtless, by nature sinful creatures. We are condemned before we have done good or evil, under the curse ere we know what it is." This is the idea of "original sin" or inherent depravity. As they are condemned before they have done good or evil, under the curse before they know what it is, then surely one is not condemned for anything they have said or done. If such be true, sin is not the "transgression of the law," but we are sinners by reason of the law of nature that brought us into existence.

Jesus says: "For the Son of man is come to seek and to save that which was lost." Lk. 19:10. According to the above theory, there was nothing for Christ to save. The elect was not lost, and the lost (non-elect) could not be saved; then there were none to save. But if Christ saved only the elect, and he saved the lost, then the elect were the only lost people on earth. On the other hand, if the elect were not lost, and Christ saved anyone, then he saved the non-elect, seeing they were the only ones lost. Again: If Christ came to save the elect only, since he came to save the lost, then the elect were the only ones lost, and the non-elect not being lost did not need a Savior!

Is salvation conditional? If I prove that it is, then the whole Calvinistic theory is false. Paul's commission was "To open their eyes [the Gentiles], and to turn them from darkness to light, and from the power of Satan unto God, that they may receive forgiveness of sins, and inheritance among them which are sanctified by faith that is in me." Acts 26:18. Note: These Gentiles were in the power of Satan, in sin. Their eyes had to be opened, they had to be turned from the power of Satan to God before God forgave them. Paul was to do this. How? "I am not ashamed of the gospel of Christ: for it is the power of God unto salvation to every one that believeth." Rom. 1:16. "It pleased God by the foolishness of preaching to save them that believe." 1 Cor. 1:21. Here are people that were not saved. It pleased God to save them by preaching. What did Paul preach? "Moreover, brethren, I declare unto you the gospel which I preached unto you, . . . by which also ye are saved, if ye keep in memory what I preached unto you, unless ye have believed in vain." 1 Cor. 15:1-2. "Believe" is a verb, in the active voice. It invariably expresses the act of man—not the act of God. Jesus says: "If ye believe not that

193

I am he, ye shall die in your sins," and "Whither I go ye cannot come." Jno. 8:22-24. The jailer inquired of Paul and Silas: "Sirs, what must I do to be saved? And they said, Believe on the Lord Jesus Christ, and thou shalt be save." Acts 16:30-31. The jailer was not saved. He was commanded to believe as a condition of salvation—a condition necessary to salvation.

I could fill pages on this subject, but another proof or two will be sufficient. "At that time ye were without Christ, being aliens from the commonwealth of Israel, and strangers from the covenants of promise, having no hope, and without God in the world." Eph. 2:12. In that condition they were certainly not saved. They were in the world, without hope, Christ or God. While in the world, they were not in Christ, hence not saved. "But now in Christ Jesus ye who sometimes were far off are made nigh by the blood of Christ." Eph. 2:13. How did these Gentiles reach the promise? "That the Gentiles should be fellow heirs, and of the same body, and partakers of his promise in Christ by the gospel." Eph. 3:6. Certainly the gospel is the means by which they were brought to the promise—to salvation.

Again: Speaking of the Jews, Paul says: "Forbidding us to speak to the Gentiles that they might be saved." 1 Thess. 2:16. These Gentiles were not saved. Paul was to speak to them that they might be saved. What was he to speak to them that they might be saved? "But as we were allowed of God to be put in trust with the gospel, even so we speak." 1 Thess. 2:4. Then Paul spoke the gospel that they might be saved. The speaking of the

194

gospel was a condition in their salvation—
sure!

SANCTIFICATION

Sanctify the Firstborn:
Ex. 13:2. "Sanctify unto me the firstborn."

Set Apart the Firstborn:
Ex. 13:12. "Thou shalt set apart unto the
Lord all that openeth the matrix, and every
firstling."

Sanctify the Lord God:
1 Pet. 3:15. "But sanctify the Lord God in
your hearts." Does this mean that we are to
make the Lord God holy—"cleanse him from
sin"? Certainly it means only that we are to
"set him apart" in our hearts.

Christ Sanctified:
Jno. 17:19. "And for their sakes I sanctify
myself."

Temple Sanctified:
2 Chr. 7:16. "For now I have chosen and
sanctified this house."

Sanctified Through the Truth:
Jno. 17:17. "Sanctify them through thy
truth: thy word is truth." Note: If people
are sanctified by the baptism of the Holy
Spirit, as some pray, then they are not sanctified in the way the Lord prayed for them to
be—for he prayed that they might be "sanctified through the truth."

Children of God Receive the Inheritance:
Rom. 8:17. "And if children, then heirs;
heirs of God, and joint heirs with Christ."

The Sanctified Receive the Inheritance:
Acts 20:32. "And now, brethren, I
commend you to God, and to the word of his

grace, which is able to build you up, and give you an inheritance among them which are sanctified." Note: 1. The children of God are heirs and will receive the inheritance. 2. But the sanctified will receive the inheritance. 3. Therefore the children of God are sanctified.

Those Forgiven Receive the Inheritance:

Acts 26:18. "That they may receive forgiveness of sins, and inheritance among them which are sanctified." Note: 1. The sanctified receive the inheritance. 2. Those forgiven receive the inheritance. 3. Therefore those forgiven are sanctified.

Church at Corinth Was Sanctified.

1 Cor. 1:2. "Unto the church of God which is at Corinth, to them that are sanctified in Christ Jesus." Note: 1. Paul addressed the church at Corinth. 2. But he addressed the sanctified. 3. Therefore the church is sanctified.

Church at Corinth Becomes Carnal:

1 Cor. 3:3. "For ye are yet carnal: for whereas there is among you envying, and strife, and divisions, are ye not carnal, and walk as men?" Note: 1. The church at Corinth was sanctified. 2. But the church at Corinth sinned by becoming carnal. 3. Therefore those sanctified may—can—become sinful.

Corinthians Sanctified by the Spirit:

1 Cor. 6:11. "But ye are sanctified, but ye are justified in the name of the Lord Jesus, and by the Spirit of our God." Note: 1. The church at Corinth was sanctified by the Spirit. 2. But the church at Corinth became carnal. 3. Therefore those sanctified by the Spirit may—can—become carnal.

Cleanse Yourselves:

2 Cor. 7:1. "Let us cleanse ourselves from all filthiness of the flesh and spirit, perfecting holiness in the fear of God." Note: 1. The church at Corinth was sanctified. 2. Paul exhorts them to cleanse themselves from filthiness of the spirit. 3. Therefore those sanctified may need to be cleansed from filthiness of the spirit.

All Men Sin:

1 Ki. 8:46. "For there is no man that sinneth not."

Eccl. 7:20. "For there is not a just man upon earth, that doeth good, and sinneth not."

1 Jno. 1:8. "If we say that we have no sin, we deceive ourselves, and the truth is not in us."

"Sanctify" means to "set apart" for divine service. Anything sanctified is set apart for God's service. The law by which things are "set apart" is the means by which they are sanctified. That which is set apart to divine service must be cleansed or purified. Jesus says: "Sanctify them through thy truth; thy word is truth." Jno. 17:17. We are set apart for divine service by the truth—the word of God. But when set apart or sanctified, we are purified. Peter says: "Seeing ye have purified your souls in obeying the truth." 1 Pet. 1:22. "The truth" is the word of God. It follows that your souls are purified in obeying the word of God. The modern Sanctificationists admit this, but say: "This only brings to pardon, but does not destroy the Adamic nature; to become wholly sanctified you must be baptized in the Holy Spirit; which destroys the Adamic nature, and leaves you without a desire to sin." Replying to such, I will say: If the Adamic nature is sin, I know you are wrong, for John says: "If we walk in the light, as he is in the light, we have fellowship one with another, and the blood of Jesus Christ his Son cleanseth us from all sin." 1 Jno. 1:7. If the "Adamic" nature is sinful, and is cleansed, it must be cleansed by the blood of Christ, for the blood of Christ "cleanseth from all sin." The Holy Spirit is not blood—never had any blood, we are not cleansed from any sin by the Holy Spirit. Paul had received the Spirit, but said, "I keep under my body, and bring it into subjection: lest that by any means, when I have preached to others, I myself should be a castaway." 1 Cor. 9:27. If all his "carnal desires" had been burned up by the Spirit, why did he have to "keep under his body" or become a castaway?

Peter was baptized in the Holy Spirit, but afterwards Paul said Peter acted a hypocrite. "But when Peter was come to Antioch, I withstood him to the face, because he was to be blamed. For before that certain came from James, he did eat with the Gentiles; but when they were come, he withdrew and separated himself, fearing them which were of the circumcision. And the other Jews dissembled likewise with him; insomuch that Barnabas also was carried away with their dissimulation." Gal. 2:11-13. What does "dissemble" mean? Webster says: "Dissemble: to hide under a false appearance; to act a hypocrite." I am sure Peter sinned grievously, and caused others to do so. Paul says of Peter and Barnabas: "But when I saw that they walked not uprightly according to the truth of the gospel." Gal. 2:14. There is not a question about the matter. Peter had been baptized with the Holy Spirit, but afterwards sinned. The beloved apostle John was baptized with the Holy Spirit, and then says: "if we confess our sins, he is faithful and just to forgive us our sins, and to cleanse us from all unrighteousness." 1 Jno. 1:9. Surely John would not teach that it was necessary for he and others to confess their sins if he did not have sins to confess—and he had been baptized with the Holy Spirit, too! This is sufficient to show that the Sanctificationists are wrong in their claim. They make the mistake in thinking the Holy Spirit is a Savior. The Spirit was never given to any person to change the nature of the person.

If Sanctificationists are right, and God expects man to live free from sin, and man cannot thus live unless baptized in the Holy Spirit, and thus has his desire to sin destroyed, since God only can baptize with the holy Spirit, who is to be blamed if man is not perfectly holy? Not man. He cannot baptize with the Holy Spirit. It must be the fault of God, seeing he refuses to give the Holy Spirit to cleanse from the desire to sin. The truth is, reader, the Sanctificationist is wrong in his contention. But they say, Isaiah says: "And a highway shall be there, and a way, and it shall be called the way of holiness; the unclean shall not pass over it; . . . but the redeemed shall walk there." Isa. 35:8-9. Every child of God is in the highway; if not, he cannot go to heaven if he should get in that way! Jesus says: "I am the way, the truth, and the life: no man cometh unto the Father but by me." Jno. 14:6. "I am the way." A man must be in Christ to be saved. "In whom we have redemption through his

199

blood, even the forgiveness of sins." Col. 1:14. Since salvation is in Christ, then you must be in Christ—the way—to be saved. But Christ—the way—must be the way of "holiness." Do you say "no"? If you do, then there must be a better way than Christ, who is the way. If you say there is another way, besides Christ, as the way, then you cannot go to heaven by that way. Why? Because Christ says: "I am the way; . . . no man cometh to the Father, but by me." Not only so, but he says: "I am the life." Then if there is another way there is not life in it. All, to be saved, must be in Christ, and as Christ is the way to reach the Father, it must follow that Christ is the "highway." Do you say: "The unclean shall not pass over it," and for that reason a man must be absolutely holy or he cannot pass into heaven? Well, if this state of holiness is brought about by the baptism of the Holy Spirit, since God can administer it, should he not do so, and then sends me to hell, who is to be blamed? Your mistake is this: You do not see how a man can be in the way, and at the same time not be able to "pass over" it. A man may be in the middle of the road that leads to town, and at the same time not be able to pass over the road, and thus go into town. He may be so drunk that he cannot "go"—pass over it. So it is in Christ, the way. A man comes into Christ; he is pardoned of all his sins. He is in Christ, the way; he walks for a while, but he is tempted; he sins. While he is in the way, he cannot pass over the way into heaven till he asks and receives forgiveness. This is why John says we must confess our sins. Christ is just to forgive our sins.

WORD OF GOD.

Worlds Were Framed By:

Heb. 11:3. "Through faith we understand that the worlds were framed by the word of God."

Heavens Were Made By:

Ps. 33:6. "By the word of the Lord were the heavens made."

Quick and Powerful:

Heb. 4:12. "For the word of God is quick and powerful."

It Gives Light:

Ps. 119:130. "The entrance of thy words giveth light."

It Gives Understanding:

Ps. 119:130. "The entrance of thy words giveth light; it giveth understanding to the simple."

It Quickens:

Ps. 119:50. "For thy words hath quickened me."

Cleansed By:

Jno. 15:3. "Now ye are clean through the word which I have spoken unto you."

Sanctified By:

Jno. 17:17. "Sanctify them through thy truth: thy word is truth."

Purified By:

1 Pet. 1:22. "Seeing ye have purified your souls in obeying the truth."

Begotten By:

Jas. 1:18. "Of his own will begat he us with the word of truth."

Born By:

1 Pet. 1:23. "Being born again, not of corruptible seed, but of incorruptible, by the word of God."

It Converts:

Ps. 19:7. "The law of the Lord is perfect, converting the soul."

Saved By:

Acts 11:14. "Who shall tell thee words, whereby thou and all thy house shall be saved."

Word of Life:

Phil. 2:16. "Holding forth the word of life."

Word of Reconciliation:

2 Cor. 5:19. "Committed unto us the word of reconciliation."

Word of Salvation:

Acts 13:26. "To you is the word of this salvation sent."

Saves Souls:

Jas. 1:21. "Receive with meekness the engrafted word, which is able to save your souls."

Spirit and Life:

Jno. 6:63. "The Words that I speak unto you, they are spirit, and they are life."

It's a Sword:

Eph. 6:17. "The sword of the Spirit, which is the word of God."

It's a Fire:

Jer. 23:29. "Is not my word like a fire?, saith the Lord."

It's a Hammer:

Jer. 23:29. "Is not my word like a fire?, saith the Lord; and like a hammer that breaketh the rock in pieces?"

It's a Seed:

Lk. 8:11. "The seed is the word of God."

It's a Lamp and a Light:

Ps. 119:105. "Thy word is a lamp unto my feet, and a light unto my path."

Be Doers of the Word:

Jas. 1:22. "Be ye doers of the word, and not hearers only, deceiving your own selves."

Keep His Word:

1 Jno. 2:5. "But whoso keepeth his word, in him verily the love of God is perfected."

Judged by the Word:

Jno. 12:48. "He that rejecteth me, and receiveth not my words, hath one that judgeth him; the words that I have spoken, the same shall judge him at the last day."

Shall Not Pass Away:

Matt. 24:35. "Heaven and earth shall pass away, but my word shall not pass away."

Rev. 22:19. "And if any man shall take away from the words of the book of this prophecy, God shall take away his part out of the book of life, and out of the holy city, and from the things which are written in this book."

Preach the Word:

2 Tim. 4:2. "I charge thee therefore before God, and the Lord Jesus Christ, who shall judge the quick and the dead at his appearing and kingdom; preach the word."

I come to the close of my little Booklet. From the above scripture you learn how God has and does instruct man for his good, and that he may spend eternity with the blessed.

Those who have not the ability to be taught are not amenable to the law of God or man; they cannot have the first conception of God or his word. They know nothing of sin or righteousness; are not responsible for their actions, and the word of God is not addressed to them. Those who have not the ability to believe have not the ability to disbelieve.

203

You know nothing of God or his will, save as you have been taught it through the medium of his word. God only knew what he wanted man to know and do; and that men might be informed as to their duty to God, as well as to their fellows, God has revealed his will through chosen persons. Such persons were not to teach more or less than God revealed; if they did, they had no right to claim they were teaching the will of God. If what men teach separate and apart from what God has revealed is the will of God, then men know the mind of God in the absence of revelation. Since man cannot know the mind of God on any subject, save as God has revealed it, you understand why we are confined to the revelation—God's word, the Bible—to learn God's will on all subjects pertaining to our life here, and the preparation necessary that we may be with him in the other life. Man cannot go to heaven by a way that he may devise; heaven is God's home, and it is his right to say who shall share that home with him. Being confined to the word of God for our knowledge of God, and his will concerning us, the importance of studying the Bible is apparent.

"We walk by faith," and "faith comes by hearing the word of God." If faith comes in any other way, then we do not walk by the faith that comes as a result of the word of God—your walk must be solely guided by the word of God. If you are not walking by faith, you cannot approach God for salvation. Since you are to approach God for salvation by faith, and faith comes by hearing the word of God, you can reach salvation by faithfully doing as the word of God says, and in that way only.

Reader, be taught of God, believe his blessed word, let it guide your life in your duty to God, and you have the assurance that you will be with him in the—end.

———————

Other Valuable Books by
C. R. Nichol

The Possibility of Apostasy

C. R. Nichol displays his extensive grasp of the Scriptures as he compares the teachings of the Bible with the denominational doctrine of the "impossibility of apostasy," or "once saved, always saved." Interesting, scholarly, revealing. 104 pages. Hardback.

God's Woman

C. R. Nichol deals with Women of the Bible, Women to Work, The Dress of Women, Custom, Subjection, Subjection in the Home, The Deaconess, and Teaching in this Scripture study. Ideal for ladies' Bible classes, God's Woman has questions and topics for discussion at the end of each section. 186 pages. Hardback.

Lord's Supper, Prayers, Thanksgivings

Bro. Nichol deals with improving prayer and communion in the worship service. A compilation of material on the Passover, the Lord's Supper, and prayer from many sources. 164 pages. Pajco softback.

Nichol-Bradley Debate

Debate with A. S. Bradley, a Materialist, on the establishment of the church and the state of the dead. Nichol called this his most memorable debate. 313 pages. Pajco softback.

Sound Doctrine, Vol. 1-5

This five-volume series of Bible studie will be an edifying addition to anyone' library. Written to be used as text books for college-level classes, guides for group Bible study, or as an outline for private study, this survey deals with fundamental teachings of the Bible, beginning with Creation. Each book contains 13 lessons with scripture references and questions for review.

Volume 1. The Bible, Creation, Adam and Eve, The Flood, The First Sermon, Disobedience, Grace, The Lord's Supper.

Volume 2. Isaac, Jacob, Esau, Joseph, Deliverance from Sin, The Ten Commandments, Prayer, The First Chapter of Acts, The Jerusalem Church, Conversion of the Samaritans, Faith, Justification by Faith, Repentance, Partakers of the Divine Nature.

Volume 3. What is the Church? Establishment of the Church, How to Become a Member of the Church, Mission of the Church, Unity, The Lord's Day, Elders, Discipline, The Sabbath, Sabbath or Lord's Day, Which?, Church Finances, Instrumental Music.

Volume 4. Divine Origin of Christianity, Nature of Man, Events of Sinai, The Tabernacle, John the Baptist, Miraculous Manifestations, The Work of the Holy Spirit in Conversion, The Heart, Conversion of the Eunuch, Actions of Baptism, Letter to the Church at Ephesus.

e 5. The Wilderness Journey, Names
...es of Christ, The Great Salvation,
Must I Do to Be Saved?, Infant
...ism, The Church at Corinth, Conversion
...aul of Tarsus, Conversion of Cornelius,
...ildiers of Christ, The Second Coming of
Christ, Eternal Life.

Sermons by C. R. Nichol

Ten of Bro Nichol's greatest: Greater
than John the Baptist, Thief on the Cross,
Saved by Grace, Why we Exist as a Church,
Never Fall, Sin Against the Holy Spirit,
Soldiers of Christ, Forgive, Unity, A Letter
from Christ. 146 pages. Pajco softback.

Nichol-Hensler Debate and
Nichol-Ballard Debate

Perhaps no other man has been more
dedicated to proving Bible doctrines than
C. R. Nichol, who participated in 363 debates
during his lifetime. Nichol debated A. A.
Hensler, a Baptist, on the establishment of
the church, and C. L. Ballard, a Methodist,
on infant baptism. Two debates in one book.
166 pages. Hardback.

A Study in Methodist Discipline

Articles of Methodist doctrine are
examined in light of the Scriptures by the
noted minister and orator who debated with
the Methodists many times. Good for
personal work, research, discussions. 64
pages. Softback.

Baptist Answers Reviewed

C. R. Nichol reviews and refutes a tract written by Missionary Baptist H. B. Taylor entitled, "Campbellite Questions and Baptist Answers." 36 pages. Softback.